When God Guides

© OVERSEAS MISSIONARY FELLOWSHIP
(formerly China Inland Mission)
Published by
Overseas Missionary Fellowship (IHQ) Ltd.,
2 Cluny Road, Singapore 1025,
Republic of Singapore

First published 1984
Reprinted 1985, 1986, 1988

OMF BOOKS are distributed by
OMF, 404 South Church Street,
 Robesonia, Pa 19551, USA
OMF, Belmont, The Vine,
 Sevenoaks, Kent, TN13 3TZ, UK
OMF, PO Box 177, Kew East,
 Victoria 3102, Australia
and other OMF offices.

ISBN 9971-972-16-6

Printed in Singapore.
cm 3K 11.88

PREFACE

The people who tell their stories in this book come from Australia, Canada, England, Germany, Ireland, Japan, Korea, Scotland, Sweden, Switzerland and the USA, as is shown by their different styles and spellings! They are a mixed bunch: men and women, older and younger, teachers, nurses, army men, ministers, students, working people — and the one thing common to them all apart from their Christian profession is that they are or have been missionaries of the Overseas Missionary Fellowship.

The subjects they write about are as diverse as themselves, including not only God's guidance to the mission field but to marriage, to houses and staff, to new types of work, in family matters of various kinds, and in the details of everyday life.

In his introductory chapter Denis Lane sets out the Scriptural teaching on guidance in ten principles, and these are "clothed in flesh and blood" as he puts it, by the stories which follow. Of course no one person's life illustrates one principle only, but they are arranged where they seem to fit most appropriately.

It is the experience of all who have written for this book that God does indeed guide. We hope that by sharing our stories with you we may encourage you to trust Him more fully.

Contents

Denis Lane *from England, joined OMF in 1960 and has worked in Malaysia and Singapore. At present he is Director for Home Ministries.*

When God Guides

GUIDANCE FASCINATES CHRISTIANS. In any church programme you can be fairly sure that the subject will come up at regular intervals. That is not surprising. If guidance is a reality, then the presence and power of God is confirmed to us. We feel assured of the supernatural world and we are confident of meaning and direction in life.

But does God guide, and does He guide individuals? Does He have a purpose and a plan for every individual life? How does He guide? Can I ever be sure that I am in the pathway of His will, and if I miss that pathway sometime, am I perpetually condemned to a second-best kind of existence? Is guidance confined to the big things of life, or must I refer everything to God's direction? These are just some of the questions we ask ourselves, each other, and God as we wrestle with the situations of life.

Guidance in this book is clothed in flesh and blood. But then God usually reveals Himself in that way. The Bible itself is the story of God revealing Himself more and more through the ages in the lives and actions of many different people. Rarely has He spoken through a voice uttering a series of words. Indeed His crowning revelation is in the form of the Word made flesh.

My job in this opening chapter is to draw out the principles which have operated through the ages in God's dealings with men and women. The rest of the book simply confirms that those principles are still alive and working today, just as God is still alive and working today. Because all the people concerned are missionaries there may be a pre-ponderance of stories about God's leading to a life's work. Obviously that is a major area where we do need to know His will. But I hope the book will show you that His concern and His guiding hand are found in many other areas of life too.

We need to remind ourselves first of all that God's primary aim for His people is to educate them for eternal life. We are predestined to be conformed to the image of His Son. He wants to make us like Christ. While therefore we may be concerned with the end result of His guidance, He is often more concerned with the teaching He can give to us in the process. For example, we are very concerned about the kind of work we shall be doing in our life. God may be more concerned with teaching us to depend on Him and to be patient in doing so. What we see as frustrating delays in hearing about our job may be the very tools that He is using to develop patience in us.

There is one other preliminary question which is important to deal with, because there is so much misunderstanding about it — the use of the word "call." We hear people say that the Lord has "called" them to do something, and frequently it is in connection with a call to so-called full-time service like being a missionary or a pastor.

In the Bible, the word "call" usually applies to the call of God to follow Jesus Christ. This is much broader than a call to a particular ministry, and it does away immediately with the idea that there are two kinds of Christians operating at two different levels. In 1 Corinthians 7:20 Paul says, "Each one should remain in the situation which he was in when God called him." "Call" here is clearly a call to follow Jesus Christ. Paul goes on to say, "Were you a slave when you were called? Don't let it trouble you." In other words, it is possible to be as good a Christian as a slave as in any other occupation. When a person becomes a Christian he often feels that he wants to give up his present work and serve the Lord "wholly". Paul is indicating that one can give wholehearted service while continuing one's present occupation. However, he goes on to say, "If you can gain your freedom do so." He is not recommending a passive acceptance of our fate, or the necessity to continue in our present occupation. He says that a Christian is free to take advantage of a better situation if that becomes available. The important point is that whether he is a free person or a slave, he is the Lord's slave and the Lord's free person. In fact he concludes "you were bought at a price; do not become slaves of men."

By confining the word "call" to people set apart by God for particular ministries we not only imply that there are two levels of Christian but we also encourage those in the "second level" to feel that they can get away with a lower level of dedication and obedience. Once we realize that the fundamental call in the Bible is to follow Jesus Christ as Saviour and Lord, all of us are subject to the same conditions of discipleship, and we all recognize that God has the right to ask us to go anywhere or to do anything at any time He chooses. The fact that the Lord directed my wife and me to serve in Asia no more relates to the level of our Christian experience or dedication than does the colour of our hair. As Christians, we are all called to serve the Lord, some in one place and some in another, some in one occupation and others in another.

How then can we know God's will, and what are the principles upon which His guidance operates? I would like to trace some principles from the Acts of the Apostles, and particularly from chapter ten which records how Peter was sent to preach to Cornelius the Roman centurion. These principles will be found worked out in the lives of the people in this book. Fortunately the Lord knows us as individual people and deals with us as such, and that is what makes the stories of His guiding hand so interesting.

Principle 1: Be prayerful

The apostles in Acts were a praying people. They often met to pray together, and even in chapter one we find them waiting upon God in prayer as they anticipated the coming of the Holy Spirit. In 10:9 we come across Peter going up on the rooftop in the middle of the day to observe a time of prayer. Peter was not seeking God's guidance when he went up those stairs to pray. He was coming into the presence of God at a normal set time of prayer for the Jewish community. But in that context he was open to receive the guidance of God.

Our modern generation has so rebelled against form and order that some Christians never have any set times for prayer. Some have said to me that they only pray when they feel like it. They seem to follow a different philosophy with their earthly meals! Our Muslim friends sometimes wonder whether we take God seriously at all. They regularly and devoutly pray five times a day, but in our reaction against formality and a mechanical approach we often limit our praying to occasional spurts of desire. Doug Vavrosky tells us how he was sure that God was sending him to the Chinese people, but the OMF leaders had reservations because of indications that he would find the language difficult. His reaction was not to struggle and push but to pray and wait, and in the end God convinced the leaders that he should go to Taiwan. Larry Dinkins was gradually brought into the

OMF as he prayed for a missionary, first alone, then in and with a group. The more he prayed, the more he learnt, until he felt compelled to be involved himself.

If we really want God's guidance, we will put ourselves in the place where He can communicate with us. In His lifetime Jesus was regular in His praying. Indeed, He was in a spirit of prayer all the time, and therefore able to be in constant contact with the will of His Father. We are told in Jude 20 to "pray in the Spirit." I do not believe this means a certain kind of praying open only to a certain kind of Christian, but constant communion between the Christian and the Holy Spirit, the Other Presence of Jesus Christ. We cannot expect God to deliver the guidance to us out of the blue if we do not cultivate His presence in prayer.

Principle 2: Let God remove your prejudices

The biggest obstacle to finding God's way sometimes lies within ourselves. Peter was a prisoner of his own cultural background: Jews never went to eat with Gentiles or they would be defiled. So before Peter could be persuaded to go to Cornelius's house, let alone preach to him, he had to have his prejudice against Gentiles removed. When God showed Peter the sheet full of unclean animals and told him to kill and eat, the hungry apostle reacted instinctively, "Surely not, Lord! I have never eaten anything impure or unclean!" This is the usual language of prejudice. When we find ourselves saying "I have never ..." or "I will never ..." about something or someone, it is more likely to be the voice of prejudice than of informed principle. Pastor Byun Jae Chang in Korea knew from the book of Jonah that God was leading him to service overseas. But God had sent Jonah to his country's enemies. In the light of past history, for most Koreans the people heading that list are the Japanese. How the Lord removed that prejudice is something to enjoy reading later on.

Parents may have to face this one when their daughter is thinking of marrying cross-culturally or cross-racially and both she and her fiancé are Christians and believe God is leading them together. Others may face it in their work when someone is promoted over them whom they feel, for some reason, should not be put in that situation. The list of possible prejudices is endless. They are especially hard to deal with if they are enshrined in the depths of our previous religious upbringing, as Peter's was. Everyone in his community felt as he did. He had been taught that that was the right way to live all his life and that it had divine sanction. No wonder the Lord had to use the special means of a vision to deal with him.

We do well to note in this connection that the Lord used the vision only to remove Peter's prejudice. He did not tell Peter where to go or what to do by means of the vision. We would much prefer guidance to be clear and specific, written in the sky or revealed in a vision. But God rarely works that way even in the era of the Spirit. The number of visions recorded in Acts is comparatively small. Again we come back to God's primary purpose to educate a people for eternity. He wants us to learn as we go along and to trust Him more and more in situations that require faith and do not have too much sight. That way we learn to walk more closely with Him. God does use dreams and visions, but only as a part of the picture, and He leaves us to think about them and to trust Him for their meaning to be revealed. Erika Heldberg-Hanser tells us in this book of two remarkable dreams that eventually had a happy ending, and Ulla Fewster's story also involves a dream. Isabel Bowman writes of a prophecy given to her at a conference which required years of waiting before it was sealed in fulfilment. In all these people's lives dreams and prophecy were but part of the picture.

Principle 3: Appreciate the value of timing and circumstances

Peter saw the sheet lowered three times. Immediately following the vision, three men who were all unclean Gentiles came knocking at his door. The Spirit told Peter to go along with them. It is not recorded exactly how the Spirit did this. Obviously Peter was sensitive to the presence of the Spirit and responsive to His prompting, but that prompting was also closely connected with the coincidence of the three-fold revelation and the three men (and I am using "coincidence" in its literal meaning and not in its modern interpretation as an accident).

When my wife and I were considering whether God was leading us overseas, three different people on separate occasions gave us their advice based on exactly the same verse of Scripture, which became our ground for approaching the whole subject. The very day we had been to London to see the OMF Candidates Secretary, a young person came into my study on our return and said, "I will not be surprised if you two go out with the OMF." She had no way of knowing where we had been.

Several testimonies in this book relate similar coinciding of incidents, that to the believer cannot be accident but come as indications from the Lord. For example, Tim Symonds writes about reading an article, receiving a letter from the OMF Home Director, and the provision of a replacement in his work, all happening at the same time. And Alice Compain knew God's guidance to move from Laos to Cambodia through incidents on three successive days.

Principle 4: Learn to recognize the voice of the Spirit

We have already seen how the Spirit told Peter to go with the men waiting downstairs. Did Peter just feel an inner compulsion? Did he hear an audible voice? We do not know. On one occasion, some years before we felt any clear leading to leave England, I was walking outside the seminary where I was studying when I seemed to hear a voice saying, "I am going to call you to a hot country."

Nothing else happened for eight years, but you cannot get much hotter than in Singapore, three degrees north of the equator. Alfred Johnston tells of being jerked alert by "a voice or an insight" which solved his bookshop staffing problem.

Many of us have experienced the leading of the Spirit in a variety of ways. Sometimes it may be more dramatic, but not necessarily so. On occasions it is a gentle prompting or a deep inner feeling. The great danger lies not in the ability of the Lord to speak to us in this way, but in our weak receptive systems. The voice of the Spirit comes to us subjectively, and in this area we are prone to make mistakes. We can so easily mistake the inner desires of our own hearts for the promptings of the Spirit. I heard someone express this recently as "baptizing our own desires". While therefore we must not ignore or play down the inner voice of the Spirit, we must be careful to test ourselves and our own sense of leading by other more objective factors too. Peter had plenty of them to go on.

What is important in this connection is that we learn to walk daily with the Spirit. If we are in constant communion with Him, practising the presence of God, then obviously we shall become more sensitive to His promptings and more able to discern between our own desires and His will. If we rarely give God a thought in the day, we can hardly expect to hear the still small voice of the Spirit in our guidance. So we have to steer a delicate course between the rationalistic unbelief that decries any inner voice of God speaking to our souls, and the emotionally heated subjectivism that lives in a constant state of tension waiting for the next inner voice. This again is a part of our spiritual education.

Principle 5: Move by faith

When the men knocked on the door Peter had to go downstairs and let them in. When the Spirit told him to go with them he had to take a journey, believing that the reason for the journey would become clear later. In any issue of guidance there comes a time for action. We cannot sit on our hands for ever debating what to do. Carolyn Blomfield admits that she needed a "sledge hammer" to get her going. But when we start moving, God can begin to open doors and to shut them. Guidance is not an infallible revelatory system that precludes our making mistakes.

Paul is a man we can all respect for the depth of his spiritual understanding and experience. He saw Christ Himself on the Damascus Road. Yet in Acts 16 we find Paul trying to go into Mysia and the Spirit telling him he was wrong. Then we find him trying to go into Bithynia with the same result. Eventually, through force of circumstances, he finished up in Troas, where the Lord gave him the vision of the man of Macedonia calling him across to Philippi. Quite clearly Paul did not have an infallible gift of guidance. Nor did he sit waiting for a revelation from heaven. He moved in the direction that he felt he should and trusted God to stop him if he was wrong. Again, in the first chapter of his letter to the Romans, Paul mentions his previous intentions to visit them on several occasions, all of which had proved abortive. However, he did not give up his plan to go to Rome because of this.

If we are uncertain what to do, whether it be in the matter of changing jobs, knowing where to invest money, when to raise an issue with a child, or any other of the thousand and one things on which we seek guidance, the time comes when we should do something. That may mean instituting inquiries about possible alternatives or seeking counsel from qualified people. It may involve writing a letter or calling at an office. God opens doors and God shuts them.

Just this week we faced a domestic situation of this kind. Our son is working in Kuala Lumpur in Malaysia and took up a new job a month ago. Since then we had not heard from him, because unknown to us a letter he had written had gone astray. We had no contact address or phone number, and were concerned to know where he was. We prayed that he would contact us, but nothing happened. So we began making inquiries with friends and contacts here in Singapore. One person who would have known our son's address had moved and changed his phone number. So we prayed and inquired. Then two days ago that very person phoned me at the office on a totally different subject. We believe the Lord moved him to do that, even though he himself may not be a believer. God had answered prayer; we learnt the truth about the letter that had gone astray, and received the information we needed. But we had to act as well as pray, trusting God to lead.

Maria Herren's story in this book shows that guidance is not always a complicated affair. We do not have to tie ourselves in knots over it. Sometimes the leading can be very straightforward, moving as it were in a straight line. Not that even this kind of guidance is without suspense in the mind of the person concerned. Maria knew what it was to have her heart in her mouth at times, but basically the way was clear to her from start to finish. The question was how it would all work out. So she went on her way step by step, trusting the Lord to unravel any complications.

Principle 6: Involve others in your guidance

When Peter set off to Cornelius' house, he asked some brethren from Joppa to go with him. That was a wise move. The Lord had removed Peter's prejudice, but plenty of people still had the same feeling against the Gentiles, and Peter wanted to be sure that he could give an account of his leading that others could confirm. He could also consult them in a time of uncertainty.

As human beings we are so prone to misinterpret the signals that we need each other to confirm our leading. Kunimitsu Ogawa's story shows the importance of this, especially to a Japanese. That is not to say that we always have to follow other people's advice. Many friends advised Paul not to go up to Jerusalem, pointing out in no uncertain terms that the result would be suffering and imprisonment. He still felt that he should go, and eventually his imprisonment brought him to the same Rome he had tried to reach several times before. Of course, we must not use this example as a excuse to persist in our own stubborn will, but advice is still advice and not a substitute for making our own decision before the Lord.

Principle 7: Be able to explain your sense of leading responsibly

Peter was able to explain to Cornelius exactly why he had felt he should go to his house (Acts 10:27–29). He could explain clearly the steps that followed each other, and the whole story made sense. Peter had been walking by faith, but faith is not irrational. Faith goes beyond reason, but does not contradict it. Peter's guidance was not entirely subjective. He had the objective fact of the arrival of the three men to account for his conclusion that he should visit Cornelius.

I sometimes get alarmed when Christians say to me with absolute confidence, "The Lord has told me to do this or that ..." but are quite unable to explain how they received that conviction. This is particularly liable to happen in matters of the heart, and understandably so, but it is also sad when a young lady feels very strongly that the Lord has told her to marry a certain person, though that person has no thought of such a relationship. Everyone gets hurt in the process. I have experienced the case of a person redirected to home ministry by more than one missionary society who nevertheless persisted in a purely subjective sense of call to go overseas. In the end she had to be repatriated by her own government because finances had run out and there was no place for her to serve. Clearly she had mistaken her guidance.

We must be careful never to set the Spirit-illuminated mind over against the other ways in which God speaks to His people. There are no superior or inferior ways of God leading. You will see in this book that some people are quite matter of fact, while others have more spectacular stories to tell. We must not set value judgments on temperaments, personalities, or ways in which people have received their guidance. I believe the principles we are considering apply universally (although not all of them in every case), but God in His grace treats us as individual people in ways that accord with our make-up. The Spirit-illuminated mind is as much a gift of God and something He uses, as is any other kind of guidance. We should therefore be able to explain clearly the reasons why we feel God is leading us to do something.

Peter in Acts 11 eventually reported back to his home church all that had happened. He had launched out into the first Jewish ministry to Gentiles — that was a fantastic new step. He needed to be able to account for why he had done it, and in the end the church endorsed it. When other people can understand our sense of guidance and endorse it as having all the marks of God's being in it, then we can feel doubly assured that we have been walking in His path. But that means we must be able to explain our leading to others in a way that makes sense to them.

Principle 8: Listen to the relevant testimony of others

When Peter arrived at Cornelius's house he was not quite sure what to do. So he explained his understanding of what had happened and then listened to Cornelius's side of the matter. The two accounts dovetailed exactly. This gave Peter the confidence he needed to preach the Gospel openly to the crowd of people in the house. Diane Davies records a remarkable instance of this kind of corroborating testimony. We do not always have anything quite so dramatic or clear on which to proceed, but when we do we can rejoice and move ahead confidently. God does deal with us as individuals, but we are not so different from others that their testimony cannot shed some light on our position, even when it does not fit our need as exactly as happened in Acts. Guidance to marriage obviously presents many examples of leading from two sides, but they are not the only ones.

Principle 9: Follow through on guidance received

Eventually there comes the time for decision. This

is different from Principle 5, because we are now thinking of the final conclusion of the matter and not just steps along the way. Eventually we have to decide where we are going to live, what school the children should attend, whether we should take up that new job, whether to accept a new commitment at church, or whatever is the question at issue. Peter reached this point in Cornelius's house and began to preach to the Gentile crowd, no doubt feeling somewhat uncomfortable as he did so. Then the Holy Spirit came down upon the congregation, and Peter did not hesitate to move from preaching to baptism, and that without prior consultation with the Jerusalem church.

When we reach a certain stage, we have to make that final decision on the evidence currently available and step out in faith that God will honour His people who are walking with Him and wanting to do His will. What we have to realize is that at this point we will not necessarily know one hundred percent that we are doing the right thing. When we hear or read testimonies of guidance such as are found in this book, we can easily conclude that these people were more sure at the moment of decision than in fact they were — that somehow they are a different kind of Christian or operate at a higher level than we do. That is a mistake. We walk by faith and not by sight right up to the end. We can only be sure we were right when we look back. Hindsight has 20/20 vision. It is this stepping out in faith even when we do not have one hundred

percent assurance that is part of the process of
God's education in our lives.

Tim Symonds saw a notice about language
training in Hong Kong, felt that language could be
a great asset in any future missionary work and
applied for the course. He was still in the Army,
and did not know for sure that it would be useful.
Today he is using that language in church planting
in Hong Kong, and can see that the decision was
spot on. At the time he made it, he did not know
whether he would go to Hong Kong or Hawaii —
he just believed God had opened a door.

Principle 10: Act in accordance with the Word of God

In drawing out these principles of guidance I have
found my source in the Word of God. There we
have recorded for us what God himself has expressed in many and varied situations. The Lord is
always consistent. What He has said He still says.
Because this is true we may depend on His Word
not only for what we should believe, but also for
principles on which we should base our lives.
Interpreted in its own literary and historical
context, the Scripture provides us with God's
illumination and direction.

So we have His promise in Psalm 32:8, "I will
instruct you and teach you in the way you should
go; I will counsel you and watch over you." The
first part of the psalm highlights both the misery of
the unrepentant sinner who holds out on confessing

his sins, and the blessedness of justification and forgiveness for the one who acknowledges iniquity and receives cleansing. Such a person becomes acutely aware of the need for guidance and direction, and that God promises to give.

We may therefore also expect that God's Word will speak to our circumstances, not only in giving us principles of guidance as it does in Acts 10 and 11, but in specific situations where we need His leading or confirmation. Let me illustrate. When my wife and I were sensing the Spirit's leading to apply to OMF for missionary service, we were encouraged by others to act on the guidance we already had. Three different people on three different days drew our attention to Exodus 33:15, where Moses, faced with the prospect of leading God's people on to the promised land, said to the Lord, "If your Presence does not go with us, do not send us up from here." That verse and its content fitted our situation as a hand fits a glove, so we were encouraged to apply to the Fellowship, praying in the same spirit.

These then are some of the principles that we see lived out in Peter's life and in many lives since then, including those in this book. We do not want to pretend that the way is always easy to discern. Anne Ruck tells of the doubts that shook her certainty of God's guidance. But Ron Preece and several others in this book testify to the peace that often accompanies a decision rightly made. Remember that Paul himself, that great man of God, made mistakes in his sense of God's leading, but he picked himself up, confident that the Lord was still going before and that eventually His will would become plain.

If we miss God's guidance, are we forever condemned to the second best? I do not believe so. The Lord is not a hard taskmaster. His yoke is easy and His burden is light. To walk in a spirit of fear that if I put a step wrong the Lord will condemn me to second-class citizenship in the kingdom of God for the rest of my life, seems to me the very antithesis of the spirit of faith that should characterize us. Remember that Peter himself on a subsequent occasion withdrew from eating with Gentiles because of the influence of other people — even after that vision (Gal. 2:11–14). Paul reproached him for his behaviour, but that was not the end of Peter's usefulness. In Jeremiah 18 the Lord showed His servant that the vessel marred in the hand of the potter could still be made into a lovely vessel. It would be a different one, but not necessarily a worse one. The world cannot forgive failure. God builds beautiful creations from ruins.

So may you be encouraged as we share our stories with you, and may all of us learn more and more to walk closely with the Lord of our lives whose guidance is promised.

Be Prayerful

Larry Dinkins *from the USA, joined OMF in 1980.*

No Blinding Light

MOST MISSIONARIES, like myself, have never seen blinding lights or burning bushes, or had a great fish to direct them into God's will. As for me, I did not sense any overpowering *call* to minister in Asia. I was simply *commanded* as are all who read this book. Although my pilgrimage to Thailand wasn't as spectacular as Paul's journey to Rome, it is none the less real to me.

Prayer

I mention prayer first since this exercise of the soul has had the greatest influence on my coming to Asia. As a second year student in seminary I was challenged to pray for a specific missionary by name. It wasn't as if missions were excluded from my prayer life, yet the subject was kept sufficiently vague to quench any effective or specific intercession. I was given the name of Dr Henry Breidenthal, president of Bangkok Bible College, and was told to pray for him daily. I was intrigued by the life of this graduate of my seminary, who was medical doctor as well as linguist, and set about lifting him up to God daily even though my knowledge of him was limited to a card with his picture on it.

In God's timing it was suggested I attend an OMF monthly prayer meeting as a way to further my growing interest in Asia. At one memorable meeting I had just poured out my heart to God for Dr Breidenthal, mentioning the problems I imagined that he and his wife and children were encountering in that Buddhist stronghold. It was then that a veteran missionary pulled me aside and gently whispered in my ear, "Larry, Dr Henry is single."

It was a lesson I was not soon to forget about the need of up-to-date, specific information concerning missionary prayer partners. James 4:3 states, "You ask and receive not, because you ask amiss ..." Surely this includes our vague requests which God may answer in a vague way.

Attending this monthly prayer meeting, meeting various missionaries, eating Asian dishes and hearing of the opportunities in Asia slowly began to erode the misconceptions which had built up in my mind concerning missionaries and missions. These prayer meetings were unlike any I had ever attended, with genuine concern shown for people removed by time and space, yet close to the Savior's heart. I am convinced that where your prayer interest lies there your heart lies also. I found it impossible to pray daily that God would meet the pressing spiritual needs in Thailand and send laborers into that harvest field, without myself becoming involved. The Lord seemed to be saying, "Larry, you can help answer your own prayer by offering yourself for service in Asia."

Now that I am nearing the end of my first term as a missionary the need for urgent corporate prayer seems even greater. What was merely theory at home has become experience in the daily grind of missionary life. It is now easy to see why missionaries write home requesting wisdom, discernment, and protection in the battle for men's souls. It is a great comfort to pull out a preaching poster knowing that 200 prayer partners are behind you in this presentation of the Gospel. In fact it is suicide to enter Satan's domain in which he has held sway for hundreds of years without men and women acting like Aaron and Hur to lift up a missionary's often weary hands in prayer.

People

As a child my conception of a missionary was a man in a pith helmet, holding a machete in one hand and a Bible in the other. Growing up in a rather liberal church, I don't remember once meeting a missionary, hearing a missionary speak or even attending a conference on the subject. A missionary was a strange bird, and the thought of eventually becoming one was as remote as the Falkland Islands. It was a great shock to learn that they come from the same bolt of cloth as myself. When you cut them they do bleed. Two such men who helped shape my life happen to have the same first name, Lewis.

Lewis McClain had been a missionary to Brazil for 12 years before having to return to Texas. As a seminarian 200 miles from mom's home cooking, I found it a real treat to share their very ample table each Sunday. Since they had only one child I became an elder son. It was Lewis who first introduced me to the excitement of ministering to inmates in jails. For him evangelism was a way to life; as we say in Texas, "He shares with anything that moves." I am indebted to Lewis for his concern for those who are usually overlooked by society, something which is important here in Central Thailand where the majority of Christians are leprosy patients.

Another man whom God used in my life is Louis Almond. Before retiring Louis and his wife Stella had a total of 71 years of missionary service, both in China and Thailand. It was Stella who first introduced me to Thai curry and Louis to the tremendous needs in Thailand. I'll never forget how he explained that Christians numbered only .1% of the 50 million population, and that Buddhist temples alone number close to 30,000 while the Christian population is a meager 60,000.

Such statistics have been used of God to move many into His fields, and they had a profound effect on me. Louis has what the Thai call a "cool heart" which is indispensable while working in the many "hot" situations which one faces. As host of the monthly OMF prayer meeting his love and godly concern for fellow workers affected not only me but countless others.

In the OMF husband and wife are accepted separately on their own merits. No wife is allowed to come in on the shirt-tails of a gifted husband. If she does she may find his shirt-tail will be cut short and both must return home. Fortunately the Lord had been preparing another 'P' for me, my wife Paula, through her involvement in a large para-church organization. As receptionist she was able to meet and become involved with many missionaries. It was a comfort to see how God had been bringing her to the point of being willing to go anywhere He led.

Concerning other family members, I must include the loving support of my parents. As an only son being groomed to inherit a sizeable business, my decision to come to Thailand must have been hard for my dad. Yet both accepted it as the Lord's will and have stood by us in prayer, even visiting the field to pray for us more effectively and understand what we are going through.

Preparation

In Luke 14:25–33 Jesus tells us to consider carefully the cost of full commitment to Christ in a life of service. "For which of you, when he wants to build a tower, doesn't first sit down and calculate the cost to see if he has enough to complete it." Having prayed and discussed with people, the final step was to calculate the cost of missionary service by careful preparation.

Upon entrance to college I had carefully calculated what it would take to become manager of a bank, and had set my sights on that goal. Meeting Christ in my second year changed all that and set me on the road to seminary. The founder of our seminary had written that the goal of seminary and of the study of God's Word should be the conversion of the nations. Yet as I looked around at our graduates it seemed that the huge majority were aiming at converting the already converted. Such an attitude was to be expected since almost all our role models were successful pastors or professors, not missionaries. Yet my degree in finance had taught me an important marketing principle. A business man doesn't flood an already overloaded market with his goods. In the small town in Oklahoma where I grew up there seemed to be a church on every corner. In Thailand I understood that there were vast areas virtually untouched for Christ. It was clear that Thailand's depressed market needed the "goods" of which America had an overabundance. Thinking in business terms, what a gold mine! Virtually no competition!

Having made the major decision to go, the next step was to prepare.

It was obviously important to familiarize myself with various mission societies. This process is similar to how God leads a person to his mate. First there is courtship, then engagement and then marriage. During the "courtship" stage I was impressed by the distinctives of OMF, especially the emphasis on prayer and their financial policies.

The preparation also means hours studying books on Thai ways and cultures, and particularly language learning. Short term missionaries are just unable to appreciate this. For us it meant one year of intensive study in the five-tone Thai tongue in Bangkok before moving up-country. Originally we were designated for Bangkok but God has a way of working through wise leaders who in this case indicated Central Thailand as the place to start. The church they sent us to is small, less than twenty believers with half semi-literate and another half leprosy patients.

Certain things are impossible to prepare for, like the five break-ins we have experienced, floods, sickness, and various disappointments. Yet the confidence that God has led us each step of the way acts as an anchor in the midst of this turbulent Thai sea. When you feel like throwing in the towel and calling it quits, God has a way of saying, "I made no mistake when I called you to Asia and it is no mistake what you are going through now. I've got everything under control, just rest in me." Obviously God is not finished with us yet, so in a sense we will always be preparing for missionary service. Orientation to the work is a constant process.

I'm very grateful to God for using prayer, people and preparation to point me in the direction of His perfect will for my life. And, frankly, that is all that really matters, whether one stays at home or goes overseas. God is the good shepherd, and His responsibility is to lead. We are the sheep of His pasture, and thus need to be sensitive to that gentle leading.

Frank Harris *first went to China in 1941, and later worked in Indonesia and Taiwan. He died in 1983.*

God Leads To An Opium Smoker

THE FIRST YEAR or two in an oriental culture can be a time of turmoil and readjustment. From being very active and perhaps successful in Christian work at home, and unfortunately sometimes lionized as one of those dedicated missionaries at the top of the Christian celebrity table, you are suddenly a nobody, useless without language, and almost alone in a sea of Chinese faces. This becomes a severe trial of faith, endurance and Christian grace, as you are tempted to irritability and to criticism of your fellow workers, who may be very different from you, perhaps a bit old fashioned, their ways of operation not what we bright, well-trained youngsters deem the best.

So it was in my first year away in a small country town in West China. My senior missionaries were devoted workers and at the top linguistically to help me with my early struggles with the language. However, as a single man I was of course an expert in children's upbringing and unfortunately my beloved seniors did not quite make the grade in child discipline! I become rather critical, and my spiritual life slumped accordingly.

One morning the Lord really convicted me of my un-Christian attitudes, and in my misery I was confessing my failures to the Lord. I told Him I had been a much better Christian back home, and perhaps He ought to send me back as a "returned empty." Just as I was confessing my sins, however, it seemed that the Lord said very clearly to me, "Go to Mr Hsieh and tell him to repent."

I was teaching a few hours of English in a local middle school, and Mr Hsieh was one of the teachers of English. He was an excellent teacher, but everyone knew he was a slave to the opium habit. I did not know him well, and did not know where he lived, but after inquiry I went round to his house. As I waited for him to come in, I noticed how bare the house was. When he entered I began with some general conversation, wondering how to approach him with the message I had come to bring. It is, after all, hardly polite to enter a teacher's residence and command his repentance. So I told him of my own failures, and how as I was confessing them to the Lord, He had told me clearly to find Mr Hsieh and tell him he must repent.

As I mentioned the word "repent" he just burst into tears. Feeling rather a hypocrite, I pulled out my Chinese New Testament and began sharing with him some of the Lord's promises of strength to overcome every weakness. Before long we were kneeling down in his kitchen, while he asked the Lord to come into his life.

From that day until the day of his death some years later he never again touched opium. His wife and children, seeing the complete transformation in his life, soon became Christians, and the family prospered.

Doug Vavrosky *from USA, joined OMF in 1981.*

The Ring
In the Nose
Technique

ALTHOUGH GOD uses many means to guide His children, such as visions, dreams and voices, I feel that the most common method God uses today is a step by step obedience to His Word. This is not a profound statement in the least, but the hard part comes in actually doing it.

How could God take a man from the North Dakota prairies and bring him to minister to the millions of needy Chinese on the island of Taiwan? How could God take a fellow set in his pattern of purposelessness and uselessness, and bestow on him the ministry of reconciliation? How could God take a complacent man blinded by the Church of Rome and give him a living, real, burning fire to serve the True Jesus within his very soul? This is nothing short of a miracle, and only by God's wonderful grace could these things, so foolish to the world, have come about.

I accepted Jesus Christ as Savior on January 1st, 1977, in a small Baptist church in my home town in North Dakota. Because of the bad company I had previously kept in that town, I knew after my conversion that the only way to get a good start in the Christian life was to move somewhere else. If you have ever been to North Dakota in the dead of winter, then it is not hard for you to realize the most logical place for me to go would be south. Therefore I spent my first winter as a Christian in Oklahoma City. It was there God started teaching me of the importance of evangelism of all types, laying the foundation for the missionary heart so needed in this lost and dying world.

On the arrival of spring I realized the importance of studying God's Word. The only problem about that was that my family and friends in North Dakota had not, to the best of my knowledge, ever learned of the riches of Christ Jesus our Lord. Therefore I went home for the summer to share this news with them before the next big move of God's leading in my life. It was while in that small country town that I realized the importance of the local church in the life of each believer, so at that time I laid the ground work of a rich supporting relationship with my home church, which is now the church that has sent me to the mission field. All this time God was keeping the desire to attend a Bible school strong in my heart.

The moment I arrived on the campus of Briercrest Bible College in September 1977 I felt a little out of place. I had never been exposed to such a totally Christian environment in my life. However, I felt that things would gradually get better. When

I had just arrived on campus, a young man named Stan encouraged me in regard to my decision to study at BBC, and he also told me of the wonderful opportunity with the missionary prayer groups. I don't know why Stan made such an impact on me, or why the Lord allowed Stan to place such a heavy burden on my heart in regard to the unevangelized in the world, especially at that particular time. Didn't God know that I was going to be busy enough studying the Bible (of which I previously knew nothing)? Didn't God know I was having enough trouble adjusting to all the Christians, with their new language I had never heard before, words like justification, atonement and sanctification? I found out this was just one more step in the program of God's guidance on my behalf — and I knew that He wasn't finished with me yet.

Missions were strong on my heart that first semester, and the first Christmas holidays I went with a team of students to Mexico with Operation Mobilization. There I was able to hear the preaching of that man greatly used of God, George Verwer. He instructed us in God's Word concerning mission day and night for two weeks straight! This also deepened my burden for missions, and intensified my concern for the unevangelized.

During this first year at Bible School the Lord was also guiding me another step along my path of discovering His will — the OMF. As I interacted with OMF missionaries and read OMF books, I was becoming more and more convinced that God was leading me to go with this mission to East Asia.

I prayed much about this and really questioned God in those early stages of my call, to see if this was really the path that God was leading me to follow. At that time my favorite place of prayer was an old dirt road that stretched for several miles down the Canadian prairie. Because I myself am a prairie boy, for me there is no place that a person can feel the nearness of God so well as in the beauty of the prairie. It was here as I walked in the early morning praying, that God confirmed His guidance to me in these specific areas: I was to go out to East Asia, and I was to go out under the OMF. Another thing that God seemed to make very clear was, "Doug, you are not to waste any time in getting out there." I don't know why God made that so clear to me, but He did.

After finishing at Briercrest, I went directly to the OMF candidate school, where I was accepted on the basis of spending a year in church work and improving my English. I completed these requirements and in the spring of 1981 went through the OMF council once again, to see if my going to East Asia through OMF actually was God's guidance after all. The council voted me in, and it was agreed that I should leave for Singapore in February 1982. But actually there was room for me to enter the October 1981 orientation course in Singapore.

Being accepted by the OMF was the final confirming step in God's guidance to get me on the mission field here in East Asia. And when I arrived at the OMF headquarters in Singapore, this was accomplished. But there was still one little matter that God had spoken to me about, way back in my first year of Bible college. To whom was I to minister?

It is truly an amazing thought, how God can take an individual from the midst of his sins and lostness, and lead him to minister to a people totally unknown to him, in an unknown land, with an unknown language. That is exactly what the Chinese people were to me. Nevertheless, as the Lord was putting on my heart the necessity to go to East Asia, He was singling out one specific group of people that He wanted me to minister to, and that was the Chinese people. I have known this from the start, but OMF didn't necessarily see it that way at first. When I applied to OMF my language ability test score was quite low, to say the least. That really ruled out the possibility of learning the complicated Chinese language. My rural background also made it less likely that I could fit into a modern urban society such as Taiwan or Hong Kong. But God had called me to minister to the Chinese — this I was sure of — and so I continued to pray and to wait.

As I departed to Singapore, my name was listed as designated to Philippines/Taiwan, with a strong push towards the Philippines. Just about halfway through my stay in Singapore, before my final designation, the directors saw it as God's guidance for me to be sent to Taiwan!

Just in case I had any doubts concerning God's guidance so far, He gave me another, even more convincing assurance that I definitely was on the right path. During my stay in Singapore I met a young South African lady by the name of Avril. She was also on her way to Taiwan with the OMF, and just happened to be in Singapore the same time as I was. I thought this was too good for words! It just so happened to be God's plan for us to be married, and to serve the Lord together in Taiwan. But what if I hadn't come to Singapore when I did, or if she hadn't come when she did? Things might not have worked out this way! I firmly believe that God's timing is a vital part in the working out of His leading. If God tells you to do something, I feel that following the Bible as a guidebook we ought to go do it, and not hesitate. Who knows how many opportunities to serve the Lord and do some good deed have been lost, all because of our sinful hesitation?

God is truly no respecter of persons. He couldn't be if He is willing to use me to carry out His work! For me His guidance has been a step by step journey in faith, waiting for God's hand to lead me through the dark places. Often the dark places are people, finances, circumstances, personal difficulties, and in my case mission boards! And so I call God's method of guiding me "The Ring in the Nose Technique." In this day and age it is hard for us to imagine how our fathers and grandfathers led the bull out to pasture. I am fortunate in being able to see this type of thing quite often in Taiwan. A farmer usually puts a big brass ring through the bull's nose, to which he can tie a rope. By this rope the bull can be pulled anywhere, day or night, wherever the farmer wants him to go. There is a remarkable resemblance between this bull and my life as a Christian. Without my really knowing why, or how, or where, God has pulled me through the experiences needed to serve Him here; and that is not to mention the blessing He has given me beside.

Hudson Taylor founder and first General Director of the China Inland Mission.

The Good, Acceptable and Perfect Will of God

> Be not conformed to this world; but be ye transformed by the renewing of your mind, that ye may prove what is that good, and acceptable, and perfect Will of God.
>
> *(Romans 12:2)*

THE VERY FACT that God is God should be sufficient to satisfy us that His will is necessarily good and perfect, and to make it acceptable to us. If infinite Love, possessed of unbounded resources and infinite wisdom, wills anything, how can that Will be other than good and perfect? And if it be not acceptable to us, does it not clearly show that we are wrong and foolish? Our position as true and loving children, redeemed at infinite cost by the mercies of God, should surely constrain us to present our bodies unto God, as living sacrifices, and practically to lay our all upon the altar for His service, seeking only to know and to do His will.

The passage before us indicates very clearly that there is a Will of the World opposed to the Will of God. Each one of us needs, with watchful care, to avoid conformity to the World's will, and to seek that spiritual transformation which will bring us into accordance with the Will of God. Theoretically, all Christians will agree with this; but practically, it is often overlooked, or insufficiently recognised.

It is an unlovely thing to see children greedily desiring to obtain all they may from their parents, but caring little to show that loving consideration and sympathy which a true parent's heart must long for. But are we, as children of God, sufficiently careful to avoid this evil? May not an unrecognised selfishness enter into our holy things, and even the Deepening of Spiritual Life be sought rather from a desire to increase our spiritual enjoyment than to be more acceptable to God or useful to our fellow-men?

If to be godly means to be Godlike; if to be true Christians means to be Christlike; if to be holy means to be conformed to the Holy Spirit of Promise, then surely we shall not be coveting the highest, but prepared to take the lowest place, if thereby we may bring salvation to the lost and ruined, wherever they may be.

Let God remove your prejudices

Byun Jae Chang *and his wife Ae Ran joined OMF in 1981.*

A Korean Jonah

WHEN I WAS YOUNG I dedicated myself to the Lord, but didn't know whether He wanted to use me or not. So I started to pray. For six months I prayed, every night for two hours. But still I did not know. At last I climbed up to the mountain to seek the Lord. It was winter and bitterly cold, but I cried out to the Lord, "What is your plan, Lord? Please, would you reveal it to me in some concrete way?"

If He did not speak, I had decided to return to the world. I had no great desire to live in poverty as a pastor, and secretly in my heart I harboured worldly ambitions.

But the Lord who said, "Call unto me and I will answer you and tell you great and unsearchable things you do not know" (Jer. 33:3), spoke to me through His Holy Spirit.

He said to me, "Go to the great city Nineveh and proclaim to it the message I give" (Jonah 3:2) and

"Set apart for me Barnabas and Saul for the work to which I have called them" (Acts 13:2).

So I made up my mind to become a pastor. But two weeks later I heard a missionary named Michael Griffiths preach from Acts 13 (my text!). Then I understood that God had called me to be a missionary — and furthermore He seemed to be pointing me to Japan. "No, Lord, not Japan. You know I dislike the Japanese!"

So from that time on the conflict began. I didn't want to be a missionary — to look a fool and sound like a baby in another language. I desired to become a great revival preacher, wonderful and respected like Billy Graham! As a result I ran away from this "call", avoiding my Lord's face ... for thirteen years!

I prayed for a compromise. "Oh, my God, instead of going myself, I will plant a church which will send out many missionaries. I will be their honoured leader." And then I went to a new industrial area and planted a church, which became the largest church in that area.

But then came a day when the Lord's hand was heavy upon me, day and night, until my strength was sapped as in the heat of summer. Finally God drove me up the mountain again. For three weeks I fasted and prayed, and I knew that I had to repent. The Lord showed me visions and spoke to my heart. Finally, I replied, "Yes, Lord; here am I, your slave. Take my silver and gold and men's applause. I will go wherever you wish".

Some time later my wife and I were greatly moved by two books — **Hudson Taylor's Spiritual Secret** and **The Life of George Muller**. If we were to be real missionaries, surely we must be spiritually qualified like these great men.

So we made up our minds to train ourselves in the life of faith. We took the financial deacon of our church into our confidence but asked him to tell no one else. He transferred our salary into the Church Building Fund and we looked to the Lord directly to supply our needs. He had given us His promises: "Open wide your mouth and I will fill it" (Psalm 81:10), and "You will drink from the brook, and I have ordered the ravens to feed you there" (1 Kings 19:4).

Hallelujah! We did open wide our mouths and He poured in everything we needed, even more than we had had before.

One day we received an unexpected visit from Dr Pattisson, OMF Superintendent in Korea. I knew of him but we had never met. And yet, although this was our first meeting, we were able to talk and testify to each other very frankly. From that day on he became my teacher, friend, counsellor and, finally, guide into OMF. When he discovered that I had been called first to missionary service 13 years before through Mr Griffiths, he told me: "The guidance of the Lord is profound. Since the visit of Mr Griffiths at that time, OMF has been praying for a Korean missionary candidate. Also for 13 years we have prayed for the establishment of an OMF Home Council in Korea. Now you and Mr Doh, who will work as secretary of the Korean Home Council, have come together, the first fruits."

As I meditated on all the Lord's dealings with me, I couldn't doubt His deep and marvellous guidance any more. With confidence I was able to sing, "I know the Lord has made a way for me."

In May 1980, Mr Griffiths came back to Korea to interview the first OMF Korean missionary candidate and to recognize the first OMF Home Council of Korea. It was a great occasion. I was the fruit of his sowing 13 years ago, and like the prodigal Jonah, had just come back into step with the Lord's perfect will.

After I repented, the Lord did in fact make me a preacher in the true sense. I went on preaching tours to several big cities and was asked to make broadcasts. I appealed to Koreans everywhere to respond to God's call to go into all the world with the Gospel. At a student conference of 2,500 I testified to the Lord's call of me, the prodigal.

My song was, "Amazing grace! How sweet the sound, that **called** a wretch like me; I once was lost, but now am found, was blind but now I see". During these preaching days, I experienced a little of the tremendous reality of that fundamental spiritual principle, "Unless a kernel of wheat falls to the ground and dies, it remains only a single seed. But if it dies, it produces many seeds."

The next question to arise was voiced by Dr Pattisson. "Where do you look forward to going?" I replied, "I will go wherever He wishes except to

Japan and Thailand. You know how we Koreans regard the Japanese. And I do not feel temperamentally suited to the Thai." Mrs Pattisson answered my hasty words: "You may have to go to Japan, Mr Byun!"

However, it seemed quite impossible for a Korean to go as a missionary to Japan. Another Korean missionary had earlier not been able to, and the response from OMF's Japan field about obtaining visas for Korean missionaries was also negative. So we put aside all thought of Japan and concentrated our preparation on Thailand. All outward signs indicated that we should go there.

Yet we lacked the inner peace and conviction that our "call" was to Thailand. In Singapore we shared our feelings frankly with the directors, who decided to postpone designation for a while. I prayed earnestly for guidance, but the Lord was silent. One day I met Wang Ting, a missionary from Taiwan serving the Lord in Japan. As we talked, I realized that her country too had suffered at the hands of the Japanese, yet she had obeyed God's call to serve there. I was clearly reminded of my initial call to Japan. Should I not be looking towards Japan after all?

"Oh Lord," I thought, "were You keeping silent because it is already fourteen years since You told me of Your will? Is Japan to be my Nineveh? Is the regulation keeping us out of Japan really unchangeable?"

Our Lord is Sovereign. He says, "Knock and ask, and the door will be opened to you!" (Matt. 7:7) So

I went to tell my conviction to Mr Lane. And the directors, our spiritual leaders, started to knock at the gates of Japan!

The Lord really did give us His perfect peace even though there was some opposition to our going to Japan. One day I thought of the words of Daniel 10:12–14, and I really felt this was given to us by the Lord. "Do not be afraid, Daniel. Since the first day that you set your mind to gain understanding and to humble yourself before your God, your words were heard, and I have come in response to them. But the prince of the Persian kingdom resisted me 21 days. Then Michael, one of the Chief Princes, came to help me, because I was detained there with the Kings of Persia. Now I have come to explain to you what will happen to your people in the future, for the vision concerns a time yet to come."

I realized that we should participate in this spiritual battle through fasting, as Daniel did. So we started fasting and prayed together. We prayed, "Lord, please send your Prince Michael to help your angel who is detained by Satan on the way to come with your answer to our prayer for the visa." About 25 days after we applied for our visa, and three days after I started to fast, we heard that our visas were granted. Hallelujah!

Willie Black *and his wife Katie, with their three children, left Scotland in 1982 to work in Korea.*

From Kinlochbervie to Korea

"KINLOCHBERVIE — where is that?" I can hear you ask. We asked precisely the same question when first we heard that name. In 1972 two happy years as assistant minister in Bathgate High Church in Scotland were drawing to a close. It was time to begin looking for a church in which I could be pastor on my own. It was an exciting but unsettling time as we waited for God to make His will plain. But how would He speak? How would He guide? Deep in my heart I knew there were prejudices which had to be taken into account, places I definitely did not want to go — to a rural or a highland parish, for example. But what I wanted did not necessarily speak of what God might want. How could we find the will of God?

My wife, Katie, and I began by making a pact with God. We would consider prayerfully before the Lord any church anywhere that expressed an interest in my becoming their pastor — in fact we would express a positive interest in them and leave it to the Lord to close the doors He did not want us to consider.

And so the day came when we were asked if we would consider the vacant parishes of Kinlochbervie and Durness. "Where is that?" we said, and nearly died with fright when we eventually found them nestling on either side of Cape Wrath in the far North West of Scotland. "But, Lord," I whispered in my heart, "You know I don't want to go to a rural and highland charge." But the pact had been made, and so our letter was mailed to say that we would consider a call to these churches.

The system in the Church of Scotland is that first of all a small committee from the vacant church will come and hear the candidate preach and will interview him. And so in due course in Fearn Abbey in Ross-shire the committee from Kinlochbervie and Durness came down to hear me preach. After the service I stood in the aisle with this little group of people and before a word was spoken between us, God Himself began to speak. It couldn't be defined but God's Spirit gave an instant and tangible oneness between us. Questions were almost unnecessary, although for the sake of formality three questions were asked before we went our separate ways. I was shaken. Had God really begun to speak? But feelings were not enough.

The next evening, late at night I shared all this with my wife. As we talked together the telephone rang — it carried an invitation from the churches in Kinlochbervie and Durness to come and be their pastor. How could we decide? Other churches were also expressing an interest in us — more desirable churches — "Lord, you know I don't want to go to a rural and highland parish — it's too small — it's too remote."

On the Tuesday morning my wife went off to work and I settled down to a quiet time before the Lord. It was with considerable trepidation that I opened my Bible at the passage for that day. I was reading in the prophecy of Nahum. Would God speak to my situation? Well, of course He did, in words of staggeringly accurate clarity. Nahum 3:18b "Your people are scattered on the mountains — they have no shepherd." God had spoken but the fight was not over. "Lord," I said, "it's the back of beyond — surely You don't want us to go so far away?" The struggle was really on, but God had more to say with the very words out of our own mouths.

The next evening Katie went off to church for a women's meeting. Because she arrived early she picked up a national church magazine to read, and found in it an article on the parishes of Kinlochbervie and Durness written by the former minister. It was the closing words, written in emphasised print, which arrested her attention "THE BACK OF BEYOND — NO, THE CENTRE OF GOD'S LOVE AND CONCERN." The struggle was over. God had spoken. Three weeks later we visited the parish and saw the truth of God's words. The people were indeed scattered upon the mountains; unlike the thousands of sheep, they were without a shepherd, and as we saw the raw barren beauty of the place we could begin to believe that it was the centre of God's love and concern.

A few months later we settled into our home there with the assurance that God knew best for our lives, and also with a strong affirmation in our hearts that we would never leave unless God spoke in just as clear a way a second time.

Eight years followed, years of learning the job of pastor, of seeing God move in many lives bringing people to Himself (in spite of much human fumbling), of experiencing the moving of God in our own lives in a new and deeper way — and of coming to a growing conviction that systematic exposition of the Word of God was the right way to preach.

Well, I guess we thought the day would come when God would move us on, but after eight years in Kinlochbervie and Durness we felt sure that such a move would still be within the confines of the Church of Scotland. We had gone far enough for God — if He moved us it would surely be south. Little did we know.

One night we had a visit in our church from OMF — Gavin Smith from Thailand and Dick Dowsett, the Scottish Secretary. First we saw Gavin's slides on Thailand and then Dick began to preach from Isaiah 42. For a preacher it is usually a great joy to sit under the ministry of God's Word. When you spend your life giving out God's Word, it is good to have the chance to drink it in. That night was no exception — but as God's Word was preached, it carried a conviction that was all the more devastating for being unexpected. It came with an almost physical heaviness as one word seemed to bear in on my soul. It was the word "nations" — the needs of the nations of the world were expounded. After the meeting, while I still reeled with the effects of God's Word, Dick casually mentioned that there was a need for Presbyterian ministers to work with the church in Korea.

Sometimes things seem to be different in the morning! The next morning I began to wonder if God had really been speaking, and so I decided to test it out. "Lord," I said, "if you really were talking to me last night, have somebody speak to me about Korea today." I felt it was a safe request. We were going on holiday that day, and I knew that we would spend nearly the whole day in our car. But that evening the impossible happened. I was helping my pastor friend dry the dishes after a meal and I shared with him the conviction of the night before. He spoke the one word I did not want to hear. "Is it Korea?" he said. I was devastated — the struggle had begun.

"But, Lord," I said — "I'm 35 — I'm too old — I've got three children — it's too many — I'll be forty before I can begin to speak the language."

It was soon Katie's turn. The first Sunday we were back in Kinlochbervie the Lord began to deal with some of the turmoil in her heart. The text that day was Genesis 46 including verses 3 & 4. "Do not be afraid to go down to Egypt — I will go to Egypt with you."

I decided it was time to talk it through seriously.

What would be involved? How did OMF work? What training would be needed? What about education for our children? On the way to a conference I called in at the OMF Scottish office, desperately hoping that a way out of it would materialize. But as Dick and I talked, shared and prayed we experienced a deep sense of the peace of God.

At the conference I asked God to speak clearly. First He gave me Hebrews 11:8,9. "By faith Abraham obeyed when he was called to go out to a place which he was to receive as an inheritance; and he went out, not knowing where he was to go. By faith he sojourned in the land of promise, as in a foreign land, living in tents with Isaac and Jacob, heirs with him of the same promise." But then on the Saturday morning I woke up with an exciting sense that God would speak that day. When it came to the evening meeting I was ready. The preacher began to speak about the need for Christians to forgive themselves for the sin that God has already forgiven — it was good but it just didn't seem relevant to the question. Was God going to miss His chance? The irreverent thought had just entered my mind when the preacher had two things to say: "There are some here tonight who must leave a work they really love and go to a completely different work — that is God's will and you must do it." Then he said, "There are some here tonight who will have to travel thousands of miles in the

will of God — that is of God and you must do it."
That was it — God had spoken.

Katie found peace in her struggle two days later
when early in the morning she read these words in a
devotional book which lay untouched by her bed,
"Glad surprises — Our Lord, we know that all is
well. We trust thee for all. We love thee increasingly. We bow to Thy will. Bow, not as one who is
resigned to some heavy blow about to fall or to the
acceptance of some inevitable decision. Bow as a
child bows, in anticipation of a glad surprise being
prepared for it by the one who loves it." Once more
God had spoken.

God does speak clearly to His children. But of
course even when He has spoken and when we
agree to do it, that does not automatically deal with
all the struggle. Even after we had decided about
Korea there was still a struggle in our hearts about
the children. If we went to Korea, the children
would have to go to school in Japan. Did God really
know what was best for our family? One day His
words came clearly to our hearts: "If it is my best
for you that you go to Korea, do you not think it is
my best for your children to go to Japan?" There
will be other struggles but there is always a God
who speaks to His people.

And so we came. The parish in Scotland had 700
people — the city of Seoul has 8 million. The
church in Kinlochbervie would see 60 people gather
on a Sunday — in churches in Seoul there are

thousands. But immense though the contrasts are, there is still a need to expound God's Word. To us the mountains we see daily around Seoul are not all that different from the mountains we enjoyed in Kinlochbervie, and certainly the God in Kinlochbervie is the same God we have found in Korea.

Appreciate the value of timing and circumstances

Alice Compain from UK, joined OMF in 1959 and has worked in Laos, Cambodia and Thailand.

Designation: Cambodia

IN SEPTEMBER 1973 I returned to England after 14 years in Laos, having worked myself out of a job. We now had five competent Lao teachers in the Bible School at Savannakhet, who had received further training in Switzerland and Thailand. I thought that perhaps I should help church elders in the villages who had never been through Bible School but were responsible for teaching and discipling. There were possibilities of producing courses for them to study at times when they were free from work in the fields.

Then out of the blue a letter arrived from OMF's Overseas Director Denis Lane, inviting me to go to Cambodia! I was asked to teach in the Bible School near Phnom Penh, in French until I could learn Cambodian.

At first I could not see that the Lord had changed my call to Laos, and it seemed that that country with its weak army would fall to the Communists before Cambodia did. I sought the advice of many colleagues and asked friends to pray. Such a big move to another country with another language to learn seemed like a mountain which I did not have enough faith to remove. I could not give an answer to the mission until I was sure that God wanted me there, and for about six weeks I vacillated, not knowing clearly what was God's will.

Then in three days the confirmation came. First, friends from Switzerland who were visiting England encouraged me to make the move before I was forty and too set in my ways. The next day I travelled to Newington Green, the OMF headquarters in London, to attend a day of prayer. Home Director Nick Carr prayed in a meeting for those who had been asked to go to Phnom Penh, obviously thinking that we had responded positively; and at the same time the Lord gave me a peace which "passeth understanding", that indeed this was His will for me, whatever the outcome. The third day I got a letter from Isaac Scott, the director in Thailand, also encouraging me that the work in Cambodia was strategic.

Now that I understood God's will, I had no option but to write back to Denis Lane accepting this new designation. We had one exciting year in Phnom Penh before having to evacuate.

Allan Crane *After 20 years in China, he also worked in Thailand before retiring in 1972.*

God leads to a horse

WE NEEDED a new pack horse. So one morning, after prayer with my wife for guidance, I visited the spring fair in Tali in Yunnan Province, China. Much cattle was for sale, cows, buffalo and horses. As I came to where the horses were tethered, I realized how little I knew about buying a horse. I stood and watched while some Chinese men looked at horses, feeling their legs and looking in their mouths. My heart failed, and I sent up a quick request for guidance. I could look into a horse's mouth but what to look for? This was going to involve quite an outlay of money and I didn't want to squander it on a broken down nag. What to do?

I went back and said to my wife, "I know nothing about buying horses. Let's pray together again that the Lord will clearly guide me." An hour or so later I sensed I should return to the fair and try again. I went, fearfully but trusting in the Lord.

As I stood again watching the horses being put through their paces by prospective buyers, I saw the Tali "hsien-chang" or county magistrate coming. I had met him once or twice and he was always courteous, listening with seeming interest to news of our work among the Lisu. But I did not want to meet him now! I walked away, but soon someone was by my side inviting me to join the magistrate's party.

He immediately asked me what I was doing at the spring fair. So I told him, "Sir, I need to buy another pack horse for our journey back to the south west."

"For that," he said, "you'll certainly need a good strong healthy horse. Do you know anything about horses?"

"We've kept horses for several years," I replied, "but I know nothing about buying them."

"I also need to buy a good riding horse and I have my 'horse doctor' here with me. He can help you find a good horse and do the bargaining for you."

"That is most kind, sir!" I said, and told him of our prayers for the Lord's guidance and help.

The magistrate followed us around looking at several horses until we came to one tall, beautiful roan. "This one is quite out of my price range", I said to myself. But the horse-doctor began his bargaining, and I could hear what an astute man he was. I felt sorry for the owner, for he was truly at a disadvantage with the magistrate standing by. The horse doctor looked over at me and asked what I wanted to pay. Then he recommenced bargaining and in a short time this horse was mine!

Erika Heldberg-Hanser *from Germany,
joined OMF in 1978 and has already spent 4 years in the
Philippines.*

Rejoice,
O daughter of
Zion

HOW I WOULD HAVE loved to go to a Christian
youth camp in summer 1970! But having just
started to train to be a nurse, I had to take my
holiday at a time when there weren't any youth
camps running. So I decided to help at an
evangelistic outreach, where they still needed some
young Christians.

After this very interesting and encouraging week,
I received a book as a sort of thank you for my help.
One member of that group said, "Erika, read this
book and you will become a missionary to the end
of the world."

So I decided not to read it, because I didn't want
to become a missionary overseas. That could mean
that I might be sent into a remote area, perhaps
into a jungle, far away from civilisation. It could
even mean staying single all my life. No, I am not
that kind of a person!

Years passed and I couldn't forget that book. At
times I hid it behind the book shelf. But this did not

help very much. I even lost my joy in reading God's Word and having fellowship with Him and other Christians. I felt more and more miserable and so one day I prayed, "Lord, I don't want to become a missionary just because that fellow prophesied it. Why can't you call me like the people you called in Bible times. Can't you speak in a similar way?"

Then I started to read that book with its bright orange cover, and got more and more relieved when I realised that the first half of the book left me quite indifferent.

One day I came in my Bible reading to Isaiah 6. I was impressed by Isaiah's immediate readiness to say, "Here am I, send me." But soon I argued, "Well, Isaiah saw God in a vision and he heard His voice audibly. In that case it wouldn't be so difficult to say, 'Here am I, send me.' If the Lord called me in such an obvious way, I would give him my life too."

Later that day I took that orange book and read another chapter. Wow me, Mr Smith mentioned on one page Isaiah 6. He wrote that this question of God, "Whom shall we send?" is not only addressed to Isaiah but also to each Christian up to this very day.

Again I argued, "No, this just can't be true. If this was the case, we would have enough missionaries everywhere!" Angrily I put that book aside and switched the radio on to relax and to think of something else. But the opposite happened. Trans-World Radio was still tuned in, and I heard the voice of a well-known German evangelist interpreting Isaiah 6! I was startled when he said, "If there is a young Christian, thinking God was only calling Isaiah in this chapter, I must tell him, he is wrong. Each Christian owes God the answer, 'Here am I, send me'."

God had chosen three different ways to make Isaiah 6 personal to me. I knew that God waited for my answer, "Here am I, send me." But still I had doubts. Wasn't I too tired and emotionally weak that day? Was it really God's voice or only men's voices? Did God want me, a little, shy nursing student, to be His ambassador? It just couldn't be!

After I had given Him my answer, I asked Him to give me a sign to prove that He really wanted me to become a missionary. And He did. How patient He was with me!

For a year after graduation I worked in a busy operating theatre. Then I enrolled at the St Chrischona Bible School and did some church work afterwards. I enjoyed working with children, young people and women, and hoped at times that the Lord would let me stay in Germany. But He kept reminding me of the many islands in South East Asia. So I became an OMF candidate and prepared myself for overseas work. I made friends with many people and also got to know some fine single fellows. But as soon as they learned that I was going to become a missionary they drew back, which sometimes hurt me very much. After this sort of experience I decided to stay single. That way I am more independent and thus can serve the Lord with my whole strength and time.

Looking back on my first four years as a single missionary in the Philippines, I can honestly say I was a very happy tribal worker and was looking forward to going back to my beloved Alangan after my first furlough. So I could not understand why, a couple of months before I was due for furlough, people asked me to think and pray about the possibility of becoming a lowland church planter. "No, I can't see that kind of work for me as a single missionary," I said quite emphatically, because I remembered the frustrations of being a constant target of Filipino fellows who hoped so much for a white wife. Often young fellows came to the Bible study only because they wanted to see me, not because of their interest in studying God's Word. Other good Filipino friends kept asking me why I didn't get married, and suggested I ought to look for a husband when I got home.

Having those experiences in mind and also the open doors we had in the Alangan tribe, I did not even want to think of furlough yet. At times I prayed, "Lord, please let me stay on at least until the end of this dry season." This request of mine was brought to the field council. Tears of disappointment ran over my cheeks when my senior missionary told me that the field council had decided I should not prolong my first term. Another member of the council took me aside, prayed with me and said, "Erika, who knows what the Lord has in mind for you during furlough? Cheer up and take this decision as part of His guidance for you."

Gradually I felt the Lord's peace flowing through

me and joy filling my heart. But when the plane took off from Manila I still could not help letting the tears flow, and prayed, "Lord, I still can't understand why I have to leave this country right now, now that I have got to love the people and to learn their language. I have only just started to be some kind of use and now you send me home. But anyway, it's good to know that you are guiding me the right and perfect way."

The four weeks holiday at home with my family helped me to forget my hesitation about going on furlough. On the whole I was looking forward to deputation work. Hadn't I a lot to report on! But when I saw the first assignment on the list, a report at my former Bible School, I became very nervous. I asked myself and the Lord, "Why do I have to start at the very place where so many know me, especially my former teachers? I would much rather have some experience elsewhere first."

While I was preparing for the talk, two other missionaries telephoned the principal and asked whether they could come that very Tuesday to speak to the students. "I am sorry," said the principal, "but we already have a speaker." If I had known of that telephone call, I gladly would have given the evening to those two missionaries. Often the principal is willing to make changes, but that day he stayed firm.

When I saw the many students and my former teachers, my knees were even more shaking. But as I went up to the platform, the Lord hadn't failed me but given strength and courage and peace. In a very natural way I was able to give my talk and show the slides.

The next morning I left St Chrischona very relieved, not knowing what had happened during the meeting to one of the students who was going to be ordained in a couple of months time. Hans-Hermann had seen my picture some months before in an OMF leaflet. And when he saw and heard me that Tuesday evening, he knew in his heart that one day I was going to be his wife.

Since the Lord had called him to missionary work overseas he constantly prayed for a wife who would be willing to go with him to the end of the world. He had even asked the Lord for a girl who had already proved this. All throughout the next week he thought and prayed over this very important matter, not without seeking advice from his counsellor.

At the same time I had a very strange and vivid dream. Now I know that the Lord wanted to prepare me through this dream. I was at a Christian rest home for one week's holiday, and in my dream I saw a car approaching the house. A young fellow asked the receptionist where Miss Hanser's room was. She accompanied him and knocked at my door, opened it and said, "Erika, there is a visitor for you." Together we went to the sitting room and then I woke up.

All day I tried to forget this dream but I couldn't, because I remembered another dream I once had in the Philippines, that one day I would enter the Calapan Mission Home with a husband. Then I went for a walk, praying, "Lord Jesus, I don't understand this dream of mine. There is no single fellow at the rest home, and I don't know of any who would have any interest in me."

The next morning I received a letter from a certain man called Hans-Hermann Heldberg, sent off in St Chrischona. In it he announced his interest to visit me soon. I was absolutely puzzled and didn't know whether I should be happy or sad. After a time of prayer I went on listening to Handel's Messiah. The very next part was "Rejoice, O daughter of Zion." To me this was an answer from the Lord.

That very evening Hans-Hermann came to me exactly in the way I had dreamed the night before.

After he had told me what had happened to him on that Tuesday, I not only remembered that dream of mine in the Philippines but also, how I once had prayed while still there "Lord, if marriage should still be your plan for my life, please 'let it happen' during one of my deputation talks."

Three months later we announced our engagement and now we are on honeymoon in Switzerland, and are looking forward to serving the Lord together for another year in Germany. And it is very likely that that dream of entering the Calapan Mission Home will become true! Hans Hermann is already an accepted OMF candidate and, if the Lord continues to guide that way, we plan to go back to the Philippines, most likely as lowland workers!

How grateful we are to the Mindoro Field

Council for pushing me on furlough at such a perfect time!

Cyril Faulkner *first went to China in 1935. He also worked in Singapore and Thailand.*

In The "Golden Years"

WHEN THE TIME CAME for us to leave Thailand in 1970 and retire, my constant question was, "What can I do with the remainder of my life?" and my continual prayer was for God's guidance.

We had not been in the USA for a week when we met some Thai ladies in a supermarket. As my wife Frances talked with them she found they lived not far from where we were staying with our daughter. So we invited them to a meal, after exchanging phone numbers.

Soon after we arrived home the phone rang, and a man's voice announced that he was the husband of one of the ladies. Could he come to the meal too, and bring a friend? When the four arrived they brought with them a large dish of curried chicken, Thai style. What a happy time we had together! We discovered that our new friend was the deputy governor for one of the Thai provinces. He had been in the USA for a year of study, and was soon returning to Thailand. He told Frances, "During the year I have met Americans in hotels and restaurants, but this is the first time I have been entertained in an American home." He invited us to his home for his farewell party. It was like being back in Bangkok. Frances made friends with a nurse, and soon they were singing "Silent Night" together in one corner. I asked one well-travelled young man what his father did. "My father is Lord Chamberlain to the King of Thailand," was his reply.

Soon we knew what God wanted us to do in reaching out to the thousands of international students and others here in the Greater Los Angeles area, a field of boundless opportunities.

Martin Dainton *and his wife, Margaret, from UK, have worked in Indonesia since 1961.*

Schools and Houses

WE HAD BEEN advised that our daughter Vivienne should not be sent at the age of 13 to the OMF hostel and English boarding school as her brother had been. So to what school should she be sent? We put out feelers to friends, because at the time alarming reports were coming through about the state of the British state-maintained schools, and they did not seem very suitable. Two or three suggestions were made, including one from a friend of Margaret's who was the deputy headmistress of a small independent girls' school in Droitwich. Her letter reached us just at the time that some decision was required, and after writing to the headmistress we agreed to send Vivienne to Dodderhill School in Droitwich, provided that we could find some accommodation nearby. It was a day school and we had no personal links with the area at all.

Time passed, inquiries made by OMF produced sympathy but not houses, and finally we arranged to visit Droitwich one Friday with OMF Regional

Secretary Ron Preece. The school term began the following week. If we could not find somewhere to live in the area that day, we did not know what to do. Various inquiries in Droitwich itself produced no result, and as Ron and we ate fish and chips in a park our hearts were sinking. After lunch we left to return to Ron's headquarters in Bristol, and as we travelled the same idea occurred to both Margaret and me more or less simultaneously. Was it worth calling on the lady with whom my cousin had lodged during a stay in nearby Worcester several years before? At least she was in the housing business, and we had met her once for about an hour, four or five years previously! Anyway, nothing would be lost by trying.

We found the house after searching our memories, and introduced ourselves. The lady remembered my cousin very well, and even me vaguely. She gave us a cup of tea and we told our tale. It so happened that her son was visiting her that afternoon, and on hearing us he said to her, "What about Roger's house?" and got busy on the telephone.

It turned out that Roger was a Baptist minister in London, who owned a house in North Worcester. That very week his tenants, some Christian nurses, were going to Australia, and he was wondering what to do about finding someone else suitable. Our new friend knew where the house was, and took us to see it. It was big enough, and not far from the main road to Droitwich, six miles away. There was a bus which Vivi could take to school.

We waited until we got back to Bristol before telephoning Roger ourselves. How we rejoiced when we heard the house could be ours for a very reasonable rent, for as long as we liked to stay!

This was not the end of the Lord's goodness. We moved in the following week, Margaret and I by car with the luggage and the children by train. Leaving the luggage at the house we went to the station to fetch them. On our return we found a total stranger cutting the lawn and his wife on the look-out for us. They proved to be members of the local church, doing a bit of tidying up for the arriving missionaries. Rick was a doctor, and his practice was in Droitwich. On hearing that Vivienne was going to school there, he immediately offered to take her every day in his car — and did so, for two years, until we returned to Indonesia.

The tale is not over yet, because having that house in Worcester introduced us to many local Christians, and our son Bernard, now at university, still regards himself as a member of the fellowship there. They have cared for and advised him, and now we are back in Asia he is eager to join in with the witness there as far as possible.

Principle **4**

Learn to recognize the voice of the Spirit

Alfred Johnston *After two years in China Alfred, who is Irish, spent 30 years in the Philippines and now works in Malaysia.*

God leads to bookshop staff

TO THE DEDICATED child of God the Lord does at times give the flash of insight and even the audible voice. We were preparing to open the third Mindanao bookshop in Butuan city, Philippines. The financial need was met and the money was on the way to us, but we still needed the other two vital components — a staff worker and a place to rent. Where would we get a suitable salesgirl? One night I was travelling home from General Santos City after helping Minda in our first branch bookshop there. I had also met her older sister, Emma, who had just returned home with a very sick husband who had been pastor in another town.

The bus was a real boneshaker and the roads were rough and potholed, so sleep was fitful. I had been praying about the need for a worker for Butuan off and on during the all-night trip. Suddenly I was jerked alert by a voice or an insight, I'm not sure which, but the message was clear,

"Get Emma for the Gen. Santos bookshop and take Minda to open Butuan bookshop."

Emma did come to us and stayed with the literature work for twenty years, later moving to Davao City and becoming overall manager of the six bookshops. Minda went to Butuan City and established the bookshop there. Later she opened bookshops in two other cities, and later still she went to Zamboanga City and not only opened the bookshop there but has managed it ever since.

Ron Preece *and his wife Kathy have been on OMF's home staff in UK since 1970.*

God
in
Control

AS I WAS halfway through my final year at school before becoming a Christian, you will not be surprised to learn that little or no prayer had gone into the question of vocation. Negotiations were well underway for me to enter the Royal Military Academy, Sandhurst — I already had the necessary academic qualifications and there remained the weekend of intelligence tests, impossible tasks set with inadequate equipment to achieve them, and interviews with the "top brass". Was the fact that Major General Pratt thought so highly of Sergeant "Tiffy" Preece, my father, significant in my securing a place at Sandhurst?

There followed two extremely happy years, six months in barrack rooms and eighteen months as a cadet. The discipline was incredibly stringent, sometimes very petty, but the training was excellent. There was so much to learn of self-control, membership of a team, principles of leadership and so on. We were honed to a fine level of physical fitness with its accompanying sense of well-being. There was ample sport of every kind for a fit young man to enjoy and a high degree of comradeship in every company. Only those who have taken part in a really high-class, large-scale parade with its precision and confidence, not to say arrogance, know what an exhilarating experience it can be. The small but active branch of the Officers' Christian Union was a great help spiritually. Of course there were frustrations, injustices, tensions and regrets, but it was an experience not to be missed and I have often reflected on it with gratitude. But as it all drew to a close I had my first encounter with the problem of God's guidance.

I had hardly stepped out, the proud possessor of the King's Commission, expecting to stay in the army until my hair turned grey, when three men, totally independently of one another, told me I should be in some form of "full-time" service for the Lord. Such a thought had never crossed my mind, but the remarkable coincidence of these three remarks stopped me in my tracks. I was confused, and this was made worse by my only attendance at the Keswick Convention. Time and again the challenge came through at the young people's meetings — "Are you prepared to go anywhere for the Lord?" I felt constrained to stand when the final appeal was made, but it was a perplexed Ron Preece who did so. What was the Lord saying? Was I reading too much into a sheer coincidence? Or was the Lord really stirring my mind and will to consider a change of purpose?

The Keswick Convention was followed by a children's camp run by the Officers' Christian Union in a lovely part of Devon. This was a totally new experience to me and I was looking forward to it with a mixture of keen anticipation and some apprehension. The camp had been running a couple of days when I arrived, and as it was early evening the campers were off on some activity or other. Another "officer" sat with me as I ate my isolated tea and I asked her what they had been doing. Among other things she mentioned the "Anchors" meeting. The children were asked whether any part of the Bible was so important to them that they could hang on to it as a ship holds to its anchor. One girl had said that she thought she would become a nurse but she wanted to be sure it was God's will. The verse that was her anchor was 1 Samuel 16:3, where God said to Samuel as he set off to anoint David, "I will show you what you shall do."

That was exactly the word from God that I needed. In His grace He had caused my friend to remember and to quote that particular verse, and through it He spoke to me and calmed all my questionings and perplexities. I was committed to the Army for three more years anyway. It was my task to be as good an officer as possible and to pray that God would open up His way for me in whatever direction it might lie.

Service in Egypt took up the next three years, and during that time there came a growing conviction that I should leave the Army and train for the ministry; so I resigned my commission.

Having come to that decision, the next question was "which college?" I knew little about any of them. As a result of talking the matter over with the Army Chaplain I wrote off to Dr Coggan, the Principal of what was then called the London College of Divinity. When my resignation had been accepted I had expected to leave the forces in July, but in fact I found myself somewhat unceremoniously jettisoned by the powers that be in May. It was the Lord's hastening, as I could now fit in an interview with the hope of starting at college for the next academic year.

On the Whit Monday I hurried away from a cricket match and crossed London to meet Dr Coggan, who then drove me down to the college in Surrey. The next morning there was time for just a brief interview before all the staff were engaged in the day's lectures. I went for a walk in the grounds before seeing the Principal again. The gardens were lovely, and as I walked around, quietly praying that the Lord's will be done, I stopped under a tree. As I did so I was engulfed in the most amazing sense of peace, assurance, well-being — how do you describe it? It was a definite physical sensation, and yet it was more. I knew then that whatever might be raised in the interview, whatever hurdles remained to be crossed, I would come and study there. And I did. Those who know me would say it was uncharacteristic for me to have such a sensation, and I must agree, but I saw it as the Lord's confirmation of His call. I had never experienced anything like it before, and was to do so only once again.

The second experience came some 18 years later. Ordination led to two-and-a-half years of happy service, and a classic example of the curate marrying the Sunday School teacher! Kathy and I probed carefully the possibility of working in East Asia with OMF. However, as Paul was prevented from going to Bithynia and was redirected to Macedonia, so our "door" to East Asia was shut and we responded to a call from Brazil.

When that period closed, we enjoyed six delightful years teaching Religious Education in the Archbishop's School in Canterbury. One Friday evening in February I had cycled home, looking forward to the half-term break. The first half of the term had passed uneventfully enough, and I sank into the fireside chair to read the post. It was then that all hopes of a peaceful evening were shattered. "We are reorganizing our H.Q. in London ..." wrote Denis Lane from OMF. "Would you consider joining us?" Our immediate reaction was to reject it, but our knowledge of the Fellowship led us to believe that such a letter would have been written only after plenty of prayer. We agreed to pray about it, and welcomed the suggestion that Denis should come down to talk it over.

That had all started on the Friday evening. On Sunday morning we took our places in church as usual. We were not expecting anything special to happen, and that is an indictment in itself! But the whole movement of the morning's service — hymns, prayers, sermon — was "Go!" Kathy and I looked at each other at the end and said, "We need a good reason for saying No!"

Denis came down ten days later as arranged, and after a careful talk together we recognized that the Lord had called us into OMF, even if it were to be a Deputation Secretary! It was as Denis left that it happened again. I was standing in the living room when there was a feeling of excitement and peace, a tingling from head to foot. It was all over in a matter of seconds, as before, but was inescapably real. Later we learned that one member of the Fellowship had been praying for eleven years that the Lord would lead us into membership.

I fancy that when our knowledge is complete "as complete as God's knowledge of me," we shall see more clearly just how wonderfully God has been in control of us and our circumstances in order to achieve His purposes both within and through us. Every day there is the constant pressure of His loving hand moving us along the road He has chosen for us. But there are the special times that we record to bring glory and thanksgiving to His Name.

Ulla Fewster *from Sweden, joined OMF in 1968.*

Coins and Dreams

WHEN I FIRST went to Thailand as a missionary, before I met my husband and joined OMF, I lived in the most horrible place I had ever seen. There was also another new missionary from Sweden, Maj-Lis Jogbrant. She had arrived in Thailand almost a year before me so her time at the Union Language School was almost up when I started there. One evening we were both invited to a monthly prayer meeting which would be my first opportunity to meet many of the other missionaries. But should we go? Neither Maj-Lis nor I knew what to do, for at ULS at that time they treated us more like sausages than people, trying to force more and more "meat" into us. If we went to the prayer meeting, which was to be held a good way from Bangkok, how could we also do our homework? So, being the spiritual girls that we were, we tossed a coin. If heads, we would stay; if tails, we would go. We tossed the coin, and it was heads — but then we realized we really wanted to go, so we went! Praise the Lord that we did!

At the prayer meeting Maj-Lis and I were introduced to two Canadian girls, Jean and Marion Bolton, who were half-time missionaries but had to support themselves by being secretaries. Top secretaries they were, too. When shaking hands with me, Marion exclaimed, "But we have met before!" I didn't think so, but for a while we both tried to think where we could have met — all without result. During the prayer meeting, however, Marion whispered to Jean, "Do you remember that dream I told you about three weeks ago?" Yes, Jean remembered. Marion had dreamed that she entered a building where several little groups of students were sitting around tables with a teacher in each group. Two of the teachers stood out in the dream, so clearly that Marion could describe them to Jean. One of them was me!

Jean and Marion didn't tell us anything about this dream, but they did invite us both to come to their home for dinner a few days later. We accepted. I can still remember — no, feel! — how I got goose-pimples on my arms when I entered that house! There was a still small voice inside me, God's voice, saying to me, "Ulla, this is where you are to live, and you are to work with these girls." I still knew nothing of Marion's dream, of course.

I said nothing to Jean and Marion that night, but I did tell Maj-Lis on the way home. "Let's go back and tell them!" she exclaimed. "No, no, how could I? Just compare their house with ours ..." I was afraid they would think I wanted a nicer house to live in! But Maj-Lis insisted that it was God's voice I had heard. "Let's pray about it for a week," she suggested. "If at the end of the week you still feel their house is the place for you, then I'll go with you and tell them."

A week later we went back to Jean and Marion's house, and with trembling fingers I pressed the door bell. Jean was at home and received us with pleasure. "Well, Jean," I said, "I might as well out with it first as last. When I was here that evening I felt as if God was telling me that this is where I am to live, and that I am to work with you."

"That's all right," said Jean. "We knew this already. We just wanted *God* to be the one to tell you." Then she told us about Marion's dream. We were amazed, and full of awe and gratitude to God.

A few days later I moved from that horrible run-down place to the beautiful house where Jean and Marion lived. I started to teach English Bible Classes at weekends and some evenings, and when my year at Language School was over I taught English Bible Classes full time.

Principle **5**

Move
by faith

Valerie Empson *from England, joined OMF in 1980.*

Folk dancing
or
Chinese?

"I WANT TO GO to folk dancing classes" was how it all started. I had a demanding teaching job in Liverpool, and was involved too at a church there. So I felt the need for some sort of relaxing activity. But the Lord's idea of relaxation and mine turned out to be two different things!

As I looked down the list to see when the folk-dancing classes were, CHINESE simply jumped off the page at me. I can't describe it any other way. I knew something had happened, yet I didn't know what to make of it. One thing I knew — my leisure time was short and therefore precious, so I needed to be sure I was going to spend it in the right way.

Having tried to dismiss the idea, without success, I turned to prayer, only willing to do something as obscure as Chinese if I was absolutely sure it was the Lord's will. As I prayed, Matthew chapter 2 came to mind and I looked it up. Some previously underlined words stared at me — words about the wise men from the East worshipping

Jesus. "I know the people of the East need to worship You," I told Him, "But that doesn't tell me to learn Chinese." Then I realized the connection. Chinese ... the East!

It seemed incredible, such a clear word, and yet I wanted to test it, I wanted practical things to fit into place too. The classes were to be on Thursdays — I wasn't free on Thursdays. I was told that that particular night school was in a very rough area and I shouldn't go alone.

Unexpectedly, a week later, Thursdays became free; and I discovered that the Chinese classes were to be held in another building, on a main road and by a bus stop! There was no turning back, I had to go on and enrol for the classes. On the first evening, I went assured by that day's Bible reading that I was to trust the Lord with all my heart and lean not to my own understanding (Prov. 3:5). Even at that stage I marvelled at all the Lord had done to ensure that I had no doubts at all, that this was of Him. There was more to come.

I would have thought the path leading towards missionary work would be one of hardship and sacrifice; but it was quite the opposite. My first faltering step of obedience led to blessing after blessing, an enriching too of my relationship with the Lord as I began to discover the secret of finding out His will — staying close to Him whatever the cost, learning to enjoy the joy and peace He gives when a life is given willingly to Him.

My six short terms at night school were fun. There were nine of us in the class, and our teacher was a Chinese who loved his people and his language. He didn't really give us an academic course, but this time proved to be an invaluable introduction to Chinese grammar, characters and the four tones. When exercises were given I did my best, knowing that it was the Lord who had put me in that class.

As time went on and I started to befriend one of the girls who was at that time deeply involved in transcendental meditation, I began to think maybe she was the reason for my being there. I conveniently forgot a promise I'd made to the Lord, "If You want me to tell the people of the East about You in any way, I will."

After three terms at night school, I was told by a close friend that she thought I was spending too much time trying to learn Chinese and was beginning to put it before other things. Did I think the time had come for me to stop going to classes?

This had never entered my mind, but I realized the Lord was using the whole incident to bring me to a point where I would turn back to Him in prayer, accepting the challenge that I'd been given. I proceeded to lay before Him all my motives for wanting to continue studying. That part was easy. It wasn't as easy to lay those motives aside and be truly willing for the alternative. Prayer became a wrestling time, but complete peace followed submission and I wondered why I hadn't been submissive earlier. All a part of growing up in the Lord!

He wasn't asking me to stop going to classes —

but He was asking me to start "opening doors" to find out why I was learning Chinese. In the past, two ministers had asked me at different times, "Have you ever thought of service overseas?" I had, but not seriously. Now was the time to see if this was a possibility.

I had met one of the OMF home staff so that was a link which made it easier to write to OMF, though I knew little about them. It was encouraging to be able to talk things over with Doug Sadler, one of the OMF regional secretaries, who told me that he felt the Lord might well be leading me into full-time service at home or overseas. He advised me to go to the annual young people's conference.

It wasn't long, however, before fears began to creep in. How would the family react? What about injections — I hate injections! And my hair! Whatever would I do with my hair if I went abroad? They were fears which I just couldn't hand over to the Lord; I clung on to them and was miserable. The fears were real, but they were groundless. There was no guarantee at that point that I would ever be going abroad at all. But the Lord understood me and simply reminded me of a song, "When we walk with the Lord in the light of His Word, what a glory he sheds on our way ..." I didn't need more, I knew I was going forward in the light of His Word and there was mention only of glory ahead, not of fears that couldn't be overcome.

I arrived at the young people's conference feeling apprehensive, wondering what the Lord had in store for me. It had been a long journey and I was thirsty. I picked up a mug to have a drink, and read on the outside of it, "The Lord your God has chosen you." I had a laugh, a quick drink and put it down! How intricately planned though are the Lord's ways. The next morning I asked Him what I should read as a beginning to the conference, and He told me Isaiah 43 — and there were the same words. "My servant, whom I have chosen." Chosen for what, I didn't know, but I knew the Lord was using these words to set a seal on all He'd been doing during the past two years.

It was suggested that I should have a Bible College course. Inside, I was indignant. I'd belonged to the Lord for twelve years, I'd been a teacher for nine years and a Sunday School teacher for longer than that. What need was there for further training? It was an OMF leaflet that challenged me, and helped me see that I had been prepared to spend three years training for secular work. Now I was to be entrusted with life's most precious Word — did I really think that I didn't need to set aside training for it? Was I prepared to go ahead into full-time service unequipped?

I recognized my arrogance, but even as I started a course at Redcliffe Missionary Training College, part of me still thought I was rather like a moulded clay pot that just needed a little painting and varnishing to be finished off! Within a short time I realized I was more like a lump of clay that was only just beginning to be moulded!

The Lord's guidance had been clear, but now there were new aspects about it to be discovered.

Within the guidance to a place prepared, there had to be an "equipping", to be ready for the steps ahead. There were times when the Lord had to slow me down and say, "Wait — I have things I want to say to you, things I want to do in you."

So that idea about folk dancing was the start of a careful five years' preparation for work overseas with OMF. Our God is a gracious God who leads us according to our personalities. He knew that although I'd been willing to go eventually, I couldn't be faced with the whole idea all at once. Instead, taking full responsibility for having sown the thought in my mind years before, He went on to lead me very simply, step by step along the path He was preparing for me.

Now, after two years of Chinese language study in Taiwan and being on the brink of doing part-time study and part-time work, I can look back over the two years here knowing that I've enjoyed them to the full. Up to this point, the culture shock I'd expected hasn't been much more than four-inch-long bananas and cats with short tails! The battles of fear I went through at home were dealt with there, and it's left me freer to start settling into a new culture, secure in the Lord's love. Of course the training still goes on, and I'm so grateful that the Lord has cared enough about me to want to bring my desire into oneness with His will.

Carolyn Blomfield *left Australia in 1977 to work as a nurse in Thailand.*

Get Going!

WHEN A NEWBORN CALF precariously scrambles onto its wobbly legs and attempts to walk, does he ask, "Hey, Mom, should I lift my left front foot first, then my right back one, then my right front followed by my left back one, or on the other hand should I begin with my right back and ...?" Surely the reply would come, "Oh for goodness sake, Junior, just WALK!"

God has given me a head with common sense to use, and much of my guidance has come from prayerfully following commonsense and asking God to shut the door if I'm wrong. Having enjoyed a precious childhood in the country I had plenty of opportunity to revel in the joy of watching young animals grow up under the guidance of their parents. Secure in the love of my own parents, I can look back now and see where they've guided and protected me at times when I was quite unaware of it. How much more able is my Heavenly Father!

I met Him during my second year of nursing

training. Some nurses whose deep security and stability puzzled me invited me along to the Nurses Christian Fellowship meetings where I first heard of the claims of Jesus Christ on my life. I struggled with the Truth for a year and finally surrendered. It then seemed common sense to continue on and finish the nursing course.

As a very new Christian the words of Luke 12:48 challenged me deeply. "Everyone to whom much is given, of him will much be required." Had not God given me a precious childhood steeped in love and security, an education, a profession as a nurse, a hundred percent health and now New Life and eternal security in Christ? Now all these tremendous privileges brought with them an awesome responsibility — how did He want me to use them? On the mission field? "Oh, no, Lord, I'm not a superspiritual giant. I'm not the missionary type, I'm just an ordinary farm girl."

Some of my nursing colleagues were of the brave, pioneering, do-it-yourself resourceful type — tailor-made for the mission field — but not me thank you very much. Reading thrilling stories of lone medical workers' adventures in the jungle was exciting so long as I wasn't wearing their shoes. No, I'd have to be assured of a definite "call" before I was prepared to venture into the wilds. Let the brave capable ones go and I'll stay at home and support them. I liked to think that missionaries were "born", their zeal for God and concern for the lost leading them straight to the mission field with never a doubt, never an apprehension. They wouldn't find it hard leaving the security of home and family and a good job. I tried to hide behind this ridiculous assumption that because I didn't "feel" like I thought a missionary should feel therefore I wasn't being "called" to be one. I secretly hoped that this was God's guidance for me.

The answer came, "Trust in the Lord with all your heart and don't rely (purely) on your own insight. In all your ways acknowledge Him and HE WILL make straight your paths ... I have made out a perfect plan for your life — are you willing to try it?"

"Yes, Lord, it's plain common sense to trust the Maker of my Life. If You want me on the mission field then I think I'm willing. I'm scared of the idea but if it is Your plan for me then please help me to be one hundred percent willing."

If ... if God was guiding me to the mission field then the common sense thing to do, I decided, was to have a basic training in general midwifery and children's nursing and then a basic biblical training. I knew I'd have to lean increasingly on my Heavenly Father when on the overseas field where there'd be no "home-props". I longed to get to know Him better so that I could lean with greater confidence. Then, too, with so much false teaching both inside and outside the church and the assurance in the Bible of an even greater upsurge before Christ returns, I wanted to be grounded in what the Bible says. Having established myself in nursing I now wanted to establish myself in the Word. That seemed to be the next logical commonsense step ...

and I'm so glad I took it. Those three years were pure gold as we explored together the richness of our inheritance in Christ.

Then the real crunch came. Basic professional training completed. Basic biblical training completed. The next step was harder — no glaringly obvious "common sense" path ahead. So now what? There were so many options.

Most final-year Bible College students seem to go through the "what does the Lord want me to do next year" agonies, and I was no exception! A lecturer had encouraged us by assuring us that God knew how to guide us each one in our own individual way. The subtle ones He'd guide subtly, whereas people who were about as subtle as a bull in a china shop the Lord knew He had to guide accordingly. I came into the second category. I am rather a skeptic by nature and don't like to trust my "feelings" and "gentle nudges" etc.

Each week at the Bible College a different mission society came to share with us the challenge of service. Certainly on common sense logistics there was a staggering inequality in today's world. The west had now so accepted as the norm its tremendous material and spiritual wealth that it was blatantly abusing its God-given privileges. "Unto whom much has been given, of him will much be required." These words were written indelibly into my being. Jesus spoke even stronger words. He said, "Go," but I felt so ordinary and I still had missionaries on a pedestal. I believe that is one of Satan's cunning weapons of deceit. How many of God's task force have stayed home because they felt so "ordinary". Come to the mission field and you'll discover just how ordinary missionaries are! Pedestals, like the tower of Babel, need to be smashed.

Gradually crawling out from the "Here am I Lord, send my neighbour" syndrome, I couldn't deny the facts. The physical and spiritual needs of so many parts of the world were crying out to be met. They were *real* people over there. How would I feel if I were in their shoes and I knew someone was able to come to help but didn't because they felt "too ordinary" to be of any use? If we met in eternity could I look them in the eye?

That was it. "I'll go, Lord," I prayed. "Thank you for making me willing. But please, Lord, which land? With whom? There are so many mission societies. How can I choose? This is my last term at Bible college, please guide me strongly, hit me over the head with a sledge hammer when I come across the mission you've chosen for me."

Two girls sharing the same struggles as I was invited me to join with them to pray together weekly for clear guidance. Oh the agony of waiting! Then one evening one of my friends announced excitedly, "God's answered, praise the Lord. He wants me in Ecuador!" We rejoiced with her and I immediately asked her how she knew. "I was reading through some mission magazines in the library when suddenly my eye fell on this article about Ecuador and I just *knew* 'that's the place for me'." While I rejoiced over my friend's answer to prayer my heart sank. "Thank you so much, Father, for giving my friend such assurance of your guidance but please Lord, I'm not as sensitive to your Holy Spirit as she is. Please guide me more sledge hammer like!"

Part way through my third term Michael Griffiths visited college explaining about OMF's ministry among East Asia's millions. Something struck a note with me — the teamwork concept — medicals, church planters, evangelists from many different nations and many different denominations united in Christ and working together for the same goal. This all appealed to me. I spoke to him privately afterwards, laying my cards on the table and explaining my fears. "I'm willing to go but don't feel adequately trained yet — what further experience did he advise?" In reply he questioned, "How old are you?" "Thirty." "Then my advice to you, young lady, is GET GOING!" I'd prayed for a hammer ... I received a hammer!

God can't guide a stationary vehicle, so taking Michael Griffiths' advice I "got going" and prayerfully filled in the primary application forms for OMF. "Lord, this is the first step of the rest of my life. I need really black and white guidance this time. If I'm not meant to be going out with OMF, then no matter how desperate is the need for nurses or how favourable my character references and checks may be, please close the OMF door so tight that no one can open it. But if I am meant to be one of their team, then no matter how unimpressed they are with me, then, Lord, open that door and let no man close it."

More agonies of waiting.

"Lord, if you were to give me a husband then I could lean on his advice, and wisdom ... I'd be willing to go wherever he felt led ... you know I hate making decisions on my own ..." "I'm your Father, TRUST ME to guide you ... I don't want you to lean on anyone else ... lean on ME ... I am your God, I will uphold you with my victorious right hand."

Eventually a phone call ... "Welcome into the OMF family ..." I remember hanging up the phone and stumbling back to my room feeling as if every last drop of blood had been drained from my veins. "Lord, they've made a terrible mistake. I'm not a Hudson Taylor ..." Then I felt another hammer blow as the Holy Spirit reminded me of my prayer. Rebuked and humbled I sank to my knees asking forgiveness for my lack of faith ... and from that moment to this I have never again doubted that OMF was His choice for me. Nor have I ever regretted making the biggest step in my Christian life — the step to the mission field. The thrills, the spills and the supreme privilege and the deep joy of being in the centre of His will are something that I'd never have wanted to miss out on. I am sometimes tempted to regret that I took so long to get out here — sitting at home shivering in my shoes instead! But the truth of the words "His timing is perfect" reassures me.

Hudson Taylor

Don't Try!

WE BELIEVE that the time has come for doing more fully what He has commanded us; and by his grace we intend to do it. Not to try; for we see no Scriptural authority for trying. "Try" is a word constantly in the mouth of unbelievers. "We must do what we can", say they; and it is far too often taken up by believers. In our experience, "to try" has usually meant "to fail". The word of the Lord in reference to His various commands is not, "Do your best", but "Do it": that is, Do the thing commanded. We are, therefore, making arrangements for commencing work in each of these nine provinces; without haste, for "He that believeth shall not make haste", but also without unnecessary delay. We hope soon to sound out the word of truth, the glad tidings of God's salvation, to the inhabitants of each of these dark regions.

Involve others in your guidance

Marianne Ritzmann *from Switzerland, joined OMF in 1970.*

In acceptance lies peace

I STAND at the train window looking out into the darkness of Central Thailand. Here and there are fires to give light to the rice-threshing farmers. Otherwise it is pitch black. This view grips my heart — it's a clear picture of the spiritual situation of the area. Here and there a few Christians, far apart, their light not always burning very brightly. The rest is deep spiritual darkness!

This is the area where I have been working for six years. I feel at home here. I love the people, and yearn for them to know the Lord Jesus! I have had many heartbreaking experiences, as people turned their backs on the Lord because of pressures from old aunts, grannies or other relatives. Yet I would love to jump off the train and continue to work here. There aren't enough church planters, we need lots more! And here I am travelling North to sit at a desk and type!

My heart is nearly torn apart. Am I really doing the right thing? Is it only common sense, or is it

God's will? After standing at the window until we leave the OMF area behind, I get back on to my bunk, disturbed, sad and confused. The battle goes on.

How have I got into this situation? I remember that it all began one day at home in Switzerland, where I had been over two years for health reasons. For months it had looked totally impossible for me ever to get back to Central Thailand. But my health had improved and I was ready to return. Then the phone rang, and to my surprise, I was speaking to my Home Director. "Two days ago I talked to a worker from North Thailand," he said. "He told me that they need a hostess for the Chiangmai Mission Home, and I thought of you, as you have gifts along this line. I have been praying about it, and have been led to approach you. North Thailand would be much better for your health than Central Thailand. I need to check with the field, but I wanted to ask you first and hear what you think about it."

"I am very surprised," I told him. "You know that my heart is in church planting, but I'll pray about it, and let you know." Feeling rather disturbed, I returned to my room.

A few months before I had told the Lord I'd be willing to go anywhere. Now I wondered, "Is it you, Lord, who wants me in the North?" Humanly speaking it made sense, but was it really God's will? After much prayer and thinking I got peace about it, and phoned my answer to the Home Director. "I'd rather do church planting, but I don't have the freedom to say 'No'. Therefore I feel it right to accept the challenge, if it is a real need."

Some weeks later, I got a letter to say that the vacancy in the Mission Home was already filled. But there was a great need in another area. The Thai Government was requiring tribal literature to be changed from Romanised to Thai script, and a typist was desperately needed for this job. The Area Director was suggesting that I should type the White Hmong Bible.

I needed to swallow twice! First, I couldn't type even in my own language! Secondly, I didn't know Hmong! How on earth would that work?

Again I took the matter up in prayer. I didn't feel equipped for the job, nor is desk work "my cup of tea". But I got peace about it, and felt compelled to accept the job, trusting the Lord to give what it takes, as He has done in the past. I found, as often before, that in acceptance lies peace.

That was three months ago, and here I am back in Thailand, travelling by night train from Bangkok through Central Thailand where my heart is, to Chiangmai, the biggest city of North Thailand.

By the time I get to Chiangmai in the morning the battle is over. I have the assurance that it is the Lord and not just the administration who wants me here. His peace floods my heart. He is leading. I want to do His will, in spite of not understanding.

For weeks I feel terribly homesick for Central Thailand, but time and time again the Lord quietens my heart. Slowly I work myself into the job, learning to type Thai, then Hmong in Thai script, a rather slow process. I learn to read Hmong, without understanding it but enough to be able to check what I have typed from a tape. Then I learn to transcribe from Romanised into Thai script. One of the things I can't get used to is the painfully slow process. It isn't easy, but the Lord provides joy and ability to get it done. I never feel bored but rather challenged every new day.

One of the sideline joys of these months is to get to know some ins and outs of tribal work. I can visit some of the stations at weekends or see my fellow workers in the Mission Home. I have been praying for them for years, now I can get to know more about them. This gives me a new urgency. The Hmong need the Bible, even if they don't like the change of script!

Slowly but steadily, one book after another gets typed. In between I am asked to relieve the Mission Home hostesses for days off or holidays. I get to love the White Hmong through short visits to one of their villages, and through their visiting us. They often turn up when they need to go to hospital, or church leaders come to discuss problems with my fellow worker, who proofreads and corrects mistakes. I am drawn towards the hardworking White Hmong people, who live in the mountains, widely scattered all over North Thailand.

By the time I start on the New Testament, I am beginning to wonder what I will be doing after finishing the typing. My health is good enough to stay on in Thailand, and my heart's desire is to be back in church planting. I know I should stay in the North, but OMF has no work among the Thai here — that means I would need to learn another language. Looking around the field I pray for guidance. After much prayer I feel compelled to go to the Hmong, in spite of common sense telling me this would be hard on my health. But I decide that if the Lord wants me there, He can see to that too. After a church service one day I surrender my life afresh to the Lord. "Lord, I am willing to go wherever, to do whatever, and go whenever — just let me know for sure what it is you want me to do."

After this I write a letter to the Superintendent to ask for a designation to the White Hmong.

Waiting for the next field council meeting is not easy, as they only happen every three months. It's a good lesson in patience! I firmly believe in corporate guidance, so I am looking forward to the decision. Just before the meeting, the Lord reminds me of my promise to go wherever! "Do you really mean it?" is His question. I am aware that there are other jobs to be done.

After field council meetings are over, the Superintendent comes and tells me that the medical report wasn't good enough for them to send me to the Hmong. He explains in a very gentle way how the Lord had led them unanimously to ask me to be the hostess in Chiangmai Mission Home. This is the home base for all tribal missionaries who work in that area, the place where they can stay when they come to town to buy food, medicine and other stores. Here they produce literature and have their team meetings, here they need to be able to share about their work, have fellowship and rest.

I know straight away that this is God's will for me, but it still comes as a great shock. For days I feel as if somebody had physically beaten me up. The question bothers me greatly: "Why was I so sure about the Hmong?" As long as I work on the Bible I can't tear my heart away from them.

After a good holiday I drive over to Chiangmai to start my new work with fear and trembling. How can I do this job well in such a international set-up? What food do I serve to Canadians, New Zealanders, British, Thai, tribal folk and all the others? What about the cultural differences? I feel very homesick for church planting and evangelism. How can I be fulfilled when I am just thinking of food, drink, shopping and cleaning all day?

It is tremendously helpful to know that people at home are praying. Never have friends written so many letters saying: "That's just the right place for you."

I experience the Lord's help no end. On many an evening I can look back surprised and full of praise to the Lord for His enabling. Many times I feel prompted to change the menu at the last minute, only to find that we have several guests more than expected and because of the Lord's leading in this way there is enough food for everybody. Many times I buy food on an inner urge and wonder afterwards why — just to find it's the Lord's provision for an unforseen need. One day I expect an empty house, but by lunch-time eleven sit around the table. I never know what will happen next, as there is no telephone even for emergencies. My fellow workers have no way to let me know ahead of time that they are coming in. That makes life interesting and helps me not to get in a rut! After the first months of struggling, I start enjoying it. Now I can say from the bottom of my heart: "The Lord has led wonderfully!"

It's amazing that the Lord should use seemingly wrong information to bring me to North Thailand. I needed a call to tribal work, to be able to cope with the many tribal visitors landing on my doorstep. Not only Hmong but Lisu, Yao and Akha come to stay overnight, especially when they or their relatives are sick. They bring messages from my fellow workers, and take mail and other things back with them.

I am very grateful for all the experience I had during my time of church planting. I know how it feels if some folks turn their backs on the Lord, I can sympathise with my fellow workers when they have to stay in town to produce literature, though they'd rather be out preaching or teaching. But somebody has to produce Bibles and hymnbooks!

I just marvel at the Lord's leading during these past years. It's very clear now: *He* planned it all! All the joy and pain was to prepare me for this job, to enable me to understand my fellow workers better. It's so much easier to pray for a situation one has been in oneself, and to encourage others who are in it.

I would never have asked to be in this job, but now I can really say that I enjoy it and feel fulfilled in it. The Lord is so good, He even provides invitations to preach in churches and enough opportunities for counselling.

His ways are so much better and higher than ours!

Kunimitsu Ogawa *and his wife Hiroko, from Japan, have served the Lord in Indonesia with OMF since 1973.*

A Great Surprise

GOD'S CALL comes always as a great surprise. It is often against our own desires or plans, and may at first seem unrealistic to our human minds. Thus our immediate reaction to it may be negative. This is exactly what happened when I was challenged with a new scheme of missionary training for Asians.

"Are you prepared to head up the missionary training scheme that we have been praying about and investigating?"

Being surprised and embarrassed, I said to the Director for Home Ministries, "No, not me! Somebody else, some experienced western missionary please!"

"I knew you would say so, but we would like you to think seriously about it."

I tried to avoid his eyes for a moment, but they gazed intently at me as if observing my embarrassment and waiting for it to die out. "I don't think I can leave the new church work in Yogyakarta, for we have committed ourselves to it for this term!" I told him.

"I have shared this already with our Area Director and superintendent in Indonesia. We in OMF will do as much as we can to help the church."

"Would it be possible to postpone the project for a few years," I asked, "until we have had some more experience or done some further studies? Actually the chairman of Japan Home Council has been asking me whether I would like to study in the United States after this term ..."

"No, we cannot postpone it," Mr. Lane replied. "We have been thinking of starting the missionary training centre at the beginning of 1985, and we would like you to be the leader. We want you to spend several months in 1984 visiting missionary training institutions in India and England, and use the rest of the year for practical preparations in Singapore."

"I am sorry," I said, "but I cannot start to think about an important matter like this just by myself. Would you please telephone to Haga-sensei, the chairman of the Home Council in Japan? If he agrees to the idea, I will think about it."

This interview took place just before the 1983 Overseas Council meetings in Singapore. I had been invited to attend the meetings to present a paper on Asian missionaries in OMF, and to comment on the discussions about the new scheme. But I had never imagined that I would be asked to lead the scheme!

As I was sitting in my room waiting for the answer to that telephone call to Japan, I felt that my inner struggle had almost reached its climax. I began to recognize that it might be wrong not to give room in my mind to serious consideration of the matter. I said to myself, "Could it be that the invitation to Overseas Council and the assignment to write this paper was a preparation for this new task?" Then there was a knock at the door. "Haga-sensei says it is OK!"

On the same day I telephoned my wife Hiroko in Jakarta. If I felt inadequate and unworthy for the new ministry, she said she felt much more so, for she was even more conscious of her lack of training. But we promised each other to pray positively about the challenge.

It is true that God's call comes as a surprise. But it is also true that He prepares our hearts for it. We begin to realize this when we are ready to accept God's call by faith. And above all God prepares His Word to confirm the call. When the new challenge came to me I was reading the first chapters of Acts again and again, because this book was to be studied throughout the Council meetings.

"'And there is salvation in no one else, for there is no other name under heaven given among men by which we must be saved.' Now when they saw the boldness of Peter and John, and perceived that they were uneducated, common men, they wondered; and they recognized that they had been with Jesus. But seeing the man that had been healed standing beside them, they had nothing to say in opposition" (Acts 4:12-14).

Here I saw two uneducated and common men boldly witnessing to Jesus Christ! I knew that Peter was an uneducated man, but I had never thought seriously that John was also. John's Gospel and his epistles reveal clearly his scholarly learning and his extraordinary personality. But the Scripture says that they were both uneducated and common men — and yet they were freely preaching the Word confidently and unashamedly. What a contrast! How could it be possible? Because they had been with Jesus, and there was the man who had been healed by Jesus standing beside them.

"Haven't I been with Jesus for the past many years? Haven't I witnessed so many men and women who have been healed by Him physically, mentally and spiritually through us? Why do I have to worry so much about my lack of formal training in theology and missionary training?"

Thinking of qualifications and responsibilities for the leadership of the missionary training scheme, I really felt my inadequacy and unworthiness. But through the Word I realized that I was wrong to think I would be adequate and worthy in the future when I had had more experience or done more academic studies. Adequacy and worthiness in God's work can never come from human qualifications, but only from the power of the grace of God accepted by faith. Thus I believed and accepted the new responsibility.

As I took this new step of faith, memories came

back to me of how the Lord had been faithful in various crises of my life. More than twenty years ago I was an atheistic student of physics. It was utterly unscientific, impossible and unnecessary for me to believe in the existence of God. And yet I was caught by the revelation of Scripture in my struggle to find the meaning of life. The simple biblical definition of sin, that we are sinners because we are far away from God, opened my heart to believe in the Redeemer. Several years later I was devoting myself to research work at an Institute of Physics in Tokyo, when the Word of God shook the whole direction of my life. "If anyone comes to me and does not hate his own father and mother and wife and children and brothers and sisters, yes and even his own life, he cannot be my disciple" (Luke 14:26,33). It seemed unrealistic and foolish to give up the prospective job. It would be against the desire of my family who had given financial support for me up to my graduate study, and would be betraying the kindness of my professor, if I followed God's call to become a full-time Christian worker. But He gave me a bold faith to surrender my will to Him for His service.

A few years later I was in Jakarta with two fellow students from the Discipleship Training Centre, Singapore. My heart was heavy because I had been asked by the OMF Home Council in Japan to think and pray about missionary work overseas. Physical and emotional problems in tropical cross-cultural community life, and mental struggles with the foreign language and the subjects of study at DTC, had given me the impression that missionary work would not fit me at all. I felt I would not come back to this part of the world! But when I was so negative and pessimistic in my thinking the words of the Lord came to me again, "Therefore I tell you, whatever you ask in prayer, believe that you have received it, and you will" (Mark 11:24). Without faith the verse is very perplexing, but once accepted by faith it reveals itself as so profound and persuasive that we cannot but accept His will. It was thus I was led into missionary service.

God's call at various stages of my life has thus made a straight line which directs my future. At each step God's grace and faithfulness have been proved. And as we go along the line of God's call we can go from strength to strength. With this conviction I have been able to face difficulties and opposition that arise after each step is taken.

"What will my church in Yogyakarta say if we tell them that we have to leave them soon? How will they react?" On my way back to Indonesia I was worried and even frightened, imagining their negative reaction. I hesitated to go back! And there was another reason for my uneasiness! I was not allowed to share the new project with my co-worker or the church people myself; our Area Director himself was to come to talk about it. At last he came. Carefully and graciously he shared about our move with our national co-worker and his wife at lunch in our house. As soon as he understood what was intended, my co-worker objected furiously! "We will not let the Ogawas go before April 1984 at the earliest! We still need them! We have just set up our programme together for the coming year. If you do this we will doubt your policy and will never sponsor OMF workers in the future!" Later he told me, "You invited us for a delicious meal, but you gave us bad news!"

Now we were in a very difficult and tense situation. We could easily understand our co-worker's feeling and reasoning. He was the dean of a seminary in Yogyakarta and also the vice chairman of the Muria Church synod which was our sponsor. But, because we had known each other for more than ten years, he had become the consultant pastor for the new church work in the town. As a result of good cooperation and part-nership between him, the church board and myself, we had begun to see some vital developments: married couples added to the originally student congregation, Javanese added to the Chinese, working people increased and church leadership and Christian fellowship strengthened. We could sense that if we left them, it would be a great blow to the congregation.

I found myself between two fires, all because we had accepted the new vision given to the OMF as a Fellowship. But I had to learn again that God's call very often puts us in such a situation. The more we try to explain to each other with words, the more we may be hurt. All we can do is wait upon the Lord in prayer.

The Area Director phoned up IHQ in Singapore and it was agreed that our move should be postponed until April 1984. But the tension was still there between my co-worker and me. I think it was two weeks after the tension arose when I visited him at his house, and he said to me, "Pak Ogawa, is it possible for OMF to send somebody else to Yogyakarta even just for a few months? If that is possible, you could go into your preparation for the new ministry as was planned originally." What a change in his attitude! At first I could not believe it! But it was true. The Lord must have been speaking to him! We praised the Lord and immediately telephoned to the Area Director in Jakarta. Several days later we had the news that another couple would move to Yogyakarta to replace us in the new year.

The Lord really blessed our team's ministry during our last three months. When 18 people were baptized in December 1983, over a hundred attended the service in the students' lodging house, compared with about 60 a year ago. Two farewell meetings, one held by the church and another by the synod, moved our hearts so that we could not stop our tears. Our co-worker is now asking for another two couples from OMF, one for theological training and the other for agricultural work.

Thus the difficulty was solved at this end. But there was another complexity coming up at the other end. The decision about our leaving Indonesia had been communicated to the Home Council in Japan through the Director for Home Ministries. But they still wanted me to go back to Japan to explain about it to the Home Council and the church leaders of my own denomination. So, after we left Indonesia, I went back to Japan for ten days. The trip was a very heavy one for it was a freezing winter in Japan, and I had to see and talk with over thirty pastors in Tokyo, Nagoya and Osaka. I was happy to find there was a good supportive understanding, and some pastors were serious in accepting this project as a new challenge for churches in Japan.

Once the step of faith is taken we can go forward, though difficulties and obstacles lie in the way. It is our testimony that our Lord has surely been with us so far. As we leave Singapore for India today, we are conscious of many other difficulties that are not yet solved: visas from the Singapore government, location of the training centre, finalizing a suitable syllabus, selection of candidates ... But we trust Him that He will remove all the obstacles and enable us to carry out His plan for the missionary training programme.

From the biography of D.E. Hoste, second General Director of the China Inland Mission.

A
High
Privilege

FOR THE SECOND TIME D.E. Hoste was checked in his desire to go to China. At first his father's refusal to allow him to resign his commission had seemed the only obstacle to be overcome. When the faith manifested in his patient waiting for God to work was rewarded, there appeared to be no further confirmation needed that it was indeed the divine will for him to go forward.

Hudson Taylor's apparent uncertainty as to whether God had really called him, however, meant that he must reconsider the whole matter. As he did so, it was impressed upon him how high a privilege it was to be called to be a missionary. Of all vocations, surely none could be greater than that of proclaiming the good news of salvation from sin and its awful penalty to those who had never yet heard of Jesus Christ! No fear of the personal sacrifice involved appears to have occurred to him, nor even misgivings as to his own ability to fulfil the commission. To the one who loves there is joy in sacrifice; and if God calls, will He not also enable? D.E. Hoste was not seriously apprehensive on either of those points. He was, however, afraid of presumption. To quote his own words, "I felt more and more the need of the utmost care and caution, lest I should presume to enter so privileged a life and service as that of a missionary in inland China, without having been really called and appointed thereto by the Lord."

In his uncertainty, he discussed the matter with various Christian friends. It must have caused him considerable inward conflict to hear the opinion again and again expressed that he should remain in the Army! The reasons given, however, never appeared to him conclusive and, like many another in a similar position he was forced back upon God, who alone could give him the assurance he was seeking.

Be able to explain your sense of leading responsibly

Isabel Bowman *from UK, first went to Japan with OMF in 1961.*

For An Appointed Time

IT WAS MARCH 24th, 1961. With a sense of excitement Lotte Mattmuller and I clambered out of our bunks and made our way up the gangway to the deck of MV Tegelberg. During the night hours we had silently sailed into Japan's waters. Early morning mists still hovered over the port of Kobe with its hundreds of tall factory chimneys belching smoke into the polluted atmosphere. Somewhere in the distance a clock was chiming the hour. Glancing upwards into the sky we glimpsed an unforgettable sight — the sun, beginning to rise in the east, seemed to hang from the mists like a huge red lantern. We had arrived at the "Land of the rising sun."

My thoughts reviewed the past nine years which had led to this special day. The "by chance" finding of the church in Oakwood, north London, where Jesus Christ became a living reality and personal Saviour. A year later, having to prepare for a youth missionary evening and needing to know about

Hudson Taylor. "Why don't you go and ask Mr and Mrs Fred Mitchell?" someone suggested. Knowing nothing of who Mr and Mrs Fred Mitchell were and still less about Hudson Taylor, I arrived on their doorstep and was kindly lent a biography. Some time later I discovered that I had been to the home of the China Inland Mission Home Director! On that evening a seed of interest was sown and the life of Hudson Taylor made a deep impression on me. "How can I find out more about this CIM?" I wondered, being far too shy to venture once more to the Mitchells' house. God had His way of seeing to that. One evening two months later the wind "happened" to blow a leaflet out of a rack in the church vestibule. That leaflet "happened" to be about the CIM Prayer Union and magazine The Millions, and led to the first of many visits to the British headquarters, then in north London.

As I still gazed out across Kobe harbour my thoughts sped on to the day when God "dropped his bombshell." Although now praying regularly for the CIM and beginning to be interested in Japan, I had never even considered actually *becoming* a missionary — my education and professional achievements were not up to such lofty standards! Then one Sunday afternoon in a little chapel on the Isle of Wight the familiar words of John Greenleaf Whittier seemed to stand out of the hymnbook in huge letters:

"In simple trust like theirs who heard

> The gracious calling of the Lord,
> Let us, like them, without a word
> Rise up and follow Thee."

The little congregation sang on, but my mind was in too much of a turmoil to continue. The "simple trust" was still a lesson to be learned. A period of questioning and argument with God ensued, but then I read 2 Corinthians 8:11-12: "If there be first a willing mind it is accepted according to that a man hath, and not according to that he hath not." There was no more to be said.

The rising sun continued its unhurried course upward into the mists over Kobe, and I pondered God's slow but sure guidance in the course of the pathway of life. First promotion and then a change of office were part of that pathway as I became responsible for the running of a small but busy Post Office. God's call to Abraham was the reminder to move on. "Get thee out of thy country and from thy kindred and from thy father's house ... UNTO A LAND THAT I WILL SHOW THEE." (Genesis 12.) This showing began with a letter headed, "If you could go to Japan and tell the Gospel story to many who have never heard how the Lord Jesus died for them — would you go?" From then onward Japan came to the land.

A hooting of sirens and much activity directed our attention to the fact that the pilot had arrived to guide us further into harbour. We had been awaiting the right conditions and timing before he could lead us on, and this reminded me how 1956 had brought the right timing to prepare to go to training college. The heavenly pilot was bidding a move on, but obstacles moved ahead too. One decisive weekend when I planned to share my desire to go to college, my brother had a minor road accident and I had a strange fall from my bicycle, causing some painful back trouble. Family pressure brought me in tears before the Lord and He reassured me from Psalm 37:5, "Commit thy way unto the Lord, trust also in Him and HE SHALL BRING IT TO PASS."

We had arrived. The pilot had brought us safely into the right place and soon we would be allowed ashore. I turned to *Daily Light* and read, "Behold I am with thee and will keep thee in all places whither thou goest and will bring thee again into this land." (Gen. 28:15). Little did I realize then how significant these words were to be in years that lay ahead. In the meantime we were content with "Behold I am with thee ..." and took our first steps onto the Land of the Rising Sun.

1965, towards the end of my first term, opened with dark clouds looming on the horizon. Letters from home hinted at concern over mother's health and especially her eyesight. My homecoming was eagerly awaited! Frequently questions arose in my mind. What will furlough bring? Suppose I have to stay home and look after both parents? How will I cope with seeing death for the first time? Just before I started packing God brought me Genesis 28:15 again. "Behold I am with thee and will keep thee ..." was sufficient answer to those fears, "and I will bring thee again into this land" was His word for a day in the future.

Another journey began. As the liner left Yokohama one January afternoon God allowed a wonderful view of Mount Fuji rising majestically into the cloudless sky. God seemed to be saying, "I will bring thee again ..." Gradually the scene changed and we sailed into the twilight and then into darkness. It was the beginning of another journey into some dark experiences of life but at that time God kindly veiled the future from my eyes.

"I'm sorry," said my mother's specialist. "There's nothing we can do for her sight. We've tested for a brain tumour but can't locate anything. Maybe six months, maybe a year will bring senility and the end." Six months passed, a year ... bringing to mother the trauma of pain from inflammation of an artery to the brain, and the emotional shock of total blindness. Though she never fully came to terms with her handicap, her strong will pulled her through, and it was a further ten years before the specialist's prophecy began to be fulfilled. Furlough extended to "leave of absence" and opinions varied as to the necessity of my remaining at home. Eventually came the heartache of resignation from OMF and adjustment to a different life. The way ahead seemed dark and gloomy. What had happened to God's promise of Genesis 28:15? "You were mistaken," came a discouraging accusation. At this time I came across the text card given to each of us new workers by George Scott, then Home

Director, when he received us into the mission. It was from Psalm 139:10-11: "Even there shall thy hand lead me and thy right hand shall hold me ... the darkness and the light are both alike to thee." With THY hand leading and holding, all must be well.

Several years passed and we had settled into a new routine. My father, though retired, worked as a bookkeeper most afternoons, and I worked in a sub-post-office each morning. Missionaries on furlough from Japan came and returned. On one occasion Doug Abrahams asked, "How old's your mum, Isabel?"

"81 years old," I replied.

"Oh, she could go on another ten years yet!" he joked.

"Another ten years!" I thought. "If that were to be so, then it's goodbye to returning for any further service."

Not long after that I attended a summer holiday conference. Quite a number of missionaries were there from various societies and were to be prayed for at the communion service. As I went to take my seat in the congregation one of the leaders spoke in my ear, "Isabel, I think you ought to sit in the front with the other missionaries and we'll pray for you too." So as hands were laid on me I was "vale-dicted" and God spoke a special prophetic word, linking up the thought of Psalm 139 and sitting in the darkness, but coming out to a place of light where fields are ready for harvest. There would be loneliness and a sword in my heart, but in a vision afterwards He spoke of feeding people with good things. In the words of Habakkuk 2:3, God confirmed in my heart that the vision is "yet for an appointed time, but at the end it shall speak and not lie; though it tarry wait for it because it will surely come."

YET FOR AN APPOINTED TIME. The next years brought my father's home call, financial testings and a personality change in my mother. Her previous cheerfulness gave way to shouting, fighting and accusations, and the distress of incontinence. Day and night I was on call, and even the district nurse who came to help could not always manage her. My back was suffering too from the weight of her heavy body. This situation continued for three years, and was worsening. I felt completely exhausted. One day I wept at the breakfast table, "Lord, please do something before long." A while later I read in Psalm 81:6, "Now I will relieve your shoulder of its burden and your hands from their heavy tasks."

Three months later a nurse called one day and, looking at me, said, "Isabel, I think you've had enough. It's time your mother was cared for in hospital." As God promised, my shoulder was "relieved of its burden" and other hands continued the heavy task until 15 months later at the age of 91 mother's weakness and suffering came peacefully to an end.

The following year, 1980, OMF called for a year of prayer for breakthrough in Japan. By then I was working in a small bank and emerging from the effects of longterm strain and tiredness. At the OMF conference that Easter, and other meetings, I kept an open ear but God didn't seem to be leading me back. "Maybe I won't be able to cope with the language and the stresses of missionary life," I thought.

Later that year the way seemed to be opening up for a holiday visit to Hong Kong the following spring. At the same time God was whispering His ideas into the hearts of some of His children. One evening my pastor said to me, "Isabel, I think you should seriously consider whether God wants you back in Japan. Will you write to OMF and explore the possibility?" Three days later as I was chatting with a deacon he said, "You have been much on my heart this past month, for I too have been wondering if God will send you back." A letter was written and wheels were set in motion.

I must confess I felt scared after posting the letter, and God, knowing that, spoke through *Daily Light* that same day, November 11th. "He led them on *safely*." He calmed my fears through the safety of corporate guidance, through the encouragement of my pastor and home church and the wisdom given to the OMF councils. A visit to Hong Kong and Japan took place in the spring of 1981 and I felt a deep sense of peace and purpose. After some study courses and hasty packing, for home was being sold, it was time for the next journey. THE AP-POINTED TIME HAD COME.

February 12th, 1982. The plane touched down at Chitose airport just outside Sapporo in the northern island of Hokkaido. There were no special "signs" for this journey. None were needed. After 17 years absence God fulfilled His promise. I WILL BRING YOU AGAIN INTO THIS LAND.

Nick Watkins *left England in 1980 to work in the Philippines.*

From Finland with Love

THERE WAS A GENERAL AIR of excitement pervading the college. The academic year was drawing to a close and the students would soon be leaving and scattering to their various homes. Some of them would be returning to their families in other parts of the world. Amidst the excitement there was not a little sadness too, since many of the students would never meet again.

My mind, however, was more or less preoccupied with one student who would be returning to her home in Finland. I had only known her about nine months and yet our relationship had grown a lot in that time. The final term had seen us grow especially close to one another, and now with the end of term fast approaching we were only just beginning to realize it!

I knew that if I wanted to reveal my feelings to Raili I would have to act soon. Yet I was not sure whether that would be the right thing to do. Raili was an accepted member of the Wycliffe Bible

Translators and I was intent on serving the Lord in East Asia with the OMF. If I spoke to her I might distract her from serving the Lord and pull her out of God's will. But if I remained silent I felt I would be treating her unfairly, and she would return home in doubt as to my true feelings and intentions towards her.

Although I was unable to see how God could be calling us together I had not completely dismissed the possibility. One evening while I was praying I had an unusual experience. It seemed as if God brought Raili's name into my mind, that He reminded me of her even though I was praying about something different. I felt as if God was saying to me, "Raili is a good friend to you and more than a friend. She would make a good wife." At that time I was unwilling to trust in this experience. I knew that such subjective guidance can be deceptive. Some good friends of mine had even married non-Christians on the basis of the feelings they experienced while praying. Such guidance on its own is not enough.

My relationship with Raili had certainly not been what I had expected of a romance. Being brought up in the "television culture" I had seen plenty of movies. Somehow I expected my romance to be a movie-type romance! I expected to fall dramatically in love with a second Miss England! On meeting Raili for the first time I registered a definite "not interested" in my mind. She was wearing a white buttoned-up raincoat and a pair of plastic rimmed spectacles that looked particularly ugly. Her appearance and my mental picture of a suitable partner did not match! I didn't know it at the time but Raili wasn't particularly impressed with me either. She still remembers the boring old-fashioned jacket that I faithfully wore every day. If she was no Miss England, I was no Mr Universe either!

Every student at All Nations Christian College is assigned to a nearby church as a part of the course. Raili and I were assigned to the same church team. Every Sunday we travelled to the church together. I helped with the young people's meeting and sometimes preached, while Raili taught a Sunday School class. It was to prove helpful to me later on in considering whether God was calling us together, to have seen Raili involved in Christian ministry. I certainly had no doubt about her walk with God.

At the end of the first term I still didn't know Raili very well. In fact, as far as making friends was concerned that first term at All Nations was a disaster. During the Christmas holidays God spoke to me about my unsociable habits, and I determined to make more of an effort to get to know my fellow students. It was not surprising that among the first people to benefit from my resolve were members of my church team, including Raili. By the end of the second term Raili and I were very good friends.

It was during the Easter holidays that the relationship began to blossom into a romance — though perhaps romance is the wrong word, since neither of us would have recognized it as such at the time. We were never aware of our friendship passing over the dividing line between friendship and love! It was during the Easter vacation that we began to correspond. Actually, when I look back I think we only started to write to one another due to a misunderstanding — perhaps a cultural misunderstanding between a Brit and a Finn!

Raili showed no signs of surprise when during the third term I became a frequent visitor to her room. She may have wondered, though, why I suddenly had such an interest to discuss college essay assignments with her, and why I always chose the times when her roommate was conveniently out. The college essays were not just an excuse, since I really wanted to know where she stood on certain key theological issues. Ours was an unusual romance in that it progressed without being detected by our fellow students. It remained a secret to the very end, which is not surprising as it was almost a secret to us as well!

As the end of term grew closer I realized it was up to me to decide whether to bring our romance into the open and talk about it with Raili, or to remain silent. In the event I chose to reveal my feelings to her. I sensed that Raili too knew why I had come and was waiting for me to bring up the subject.

"Raili, I feel I ought to tell you that I like you very much, but there is no future for our relationship." For a moment we were both silent. "Well, what do you think?" I asked.

"I think things are not quite as black and white

as you make them out to be," she said quietly, with an obvious tone of excitement in her voice.

In the end we decided to continue to get to know one another better, while at the same time earnestly seeking the will of God for our lives. What Raili had said was true, things were not quite so black and white as I had imagined. We may have been committed to different missionary societies, but we were both committed to the Lord and to serving Him in another country.

At the end of term Raili returned home to Finland and I returned home to Bristol. We wrote to one another and continued to pray to the Lord. For me it was a very difficult situation. I felt lost without a sure guide, at the mercy of my feelings. I knew the Bible forbad the marriage of a Christian to a non-Christian, but it had nothing to say about marrying a girl from another missionary society.

But God spoke to me clearly in my need. It happened while I was enjoying a caravan holiday in Scotland with some friends from my church. Sometimes I would go for a walk on my own and find a secluded spot where I could talk to the Lord and read the Scriptures. On this occasion I sat facing the setting sun. There was an island offshore and the sun was sinking behind it. As the sun disappeared, a streak of rippling redness began to cross the sea towards me. As I watched this beautiful sight a sense of awe and of God's wonder came over me. I realized a little of the beauty and greatness of God. Did I not believe in this same sovereign God who controlled the rising and the setting of the sun? Surely I could trust Him to guide me! He who upholds the universe and guides the stars in their paths neither lacks the ability nor the desire to guide His children. At that time I put my trust in God that He would not let me go astray but would correct me if I went wrong.

While I was struggling with my feelings, Raili too was grappling with hers. She was confused. Before I arrived on the scene the future had been fairly clear and straightforward. Why had God led her to join Wycliffe Bible Translators if it was His will that she should marry me? God never makes mistakes, but had she made a mistake? She had known God's clear guidance in applying to Wycliffe, there was no doubt in her mind about that. In fact it was they who had recommended that she go to All Nations Christian College for a further year's training. Could it be that in God's mysterious will this was the route He had planned for her to find the man He had chosen for her?

Towards the end of the term something happened that helped Raili to see God's hand at work in her situation. The students met together to pray and to share, and one read from Jeremiah 29:11: "'I know the plans I have for you,' declares the Lord, 'plans to prosper you and not to harm you, plans to give you a future and a hope.'" Raili was confused but God wasn't. He knew the plans He had for her. Jeremiah's words became a star of hope that shone through the perplexing days of separation that followed.

Also Raili began to realize that the real question she had to answer was whether God was leading her to marry me. If He was, He was also calling her to follow me. Once she was sure of God's call to marriage, following her husband in joining OMF became no problem.

As we both sought God's will for our future, I in England and Raili in Finland, it became clear to us both that God had led us together so that we might serve Him as man and wife. We were both surprised by God's goodness to us. In His love He had planned it all. How else could we have met one another and got to know each other? God had bridged the obstacles that separated us geographically and linguistically; He had even found a way around my shyness!

Both Raili and I had come to the point where we were willing to serve the Lord as single people. Raili knew when she joined Wycliffe Bible Translators that her chances of getting a husband were slim. Who would be interested in marrying her except another Wycliffe member? And there aren't many bachelors around in Wycliffe, as is the case in most other missionary societies. I for my part had had a strong desire to get married ever since I left university. It was only at All Nations that I had realized that I could be happy serving the Lord as a bachelor. The realistic teaching at the college helped me to see that married life is not all a bed of roses. Married persons as well as single people have problems, only of a different kind. Psalm 84:11 became very precious to me, "For the Lord God is a sun and shield; the Lord will give grace and glory. No good thing will he withhold from them that walk uprightly."

If the Lord felt it was good for me to marry he would provide me with a wife; if not He would give me the joy of serving Him as a single person. And in His goodness He chose the path of married life for me.

Principle **8**

Listen to the relevant testimony of others

Diane Davies *from Canada, has worked in both Thailand and Malaysia.*

Gold Tried In The Fire

IN THE SPRING OF 1969, I left Canada for Singapore to become a foreign missionary. I had had several years of training and thought I was ready to "convert the heathen" some place in South East Asia.

During interviews with directors at our International Headquarters, I was asked if I would be willing to teach missionaries' children at Chefoo School in Malaysia. I was shattered by this suggestion. I thought that missionary kids were not particularly important, and if I had wanted to teach western children I would have stayed in Canada. The idea of a boarding school filled me with dread. How could God ask parents to send their children hundreds of miles away from home for eighteen weeks at a time! It was cruel and inhuman. Besides, I had come to do "real" missionary work, not to babysit missionary kids. Therefore, I told the directors, I was definitely not willing to go to Chefoo.

I was then sent to Thailand with the idea of doing student work. But God had other ideas of His own for me as He patiently taught me many valuable lessons while in Thailand.

First I had to learn from where my security comes. I really believed that I trusted God for all things, but I quickly learned that my security came not from God, but from my family, my church, my language, my culture and customs. When these were all removed, my sense of security evaporated. For the first time in my life, I had to depend on God and on Him alone for my security.

I also had to learn that problems and trials come from a loving Father who is making me more like His Son, Jesus Christ. On arriving in Thailand I was hit with dengue fever — a nasty mosquito bit me — and amoebic dysentery — someone gave me a contaminated glass of water when I fainted from the heat. My first year was spent in and out of bed, trying to cope with poor health, language school and a new culture.

After many months of this I was ready to give up the struggle, and on June 19th I wrote my resignation to OMF and left it on my desk to post in the morning.

For many years, it has been my habit to read "Daily Light" before I go to sleep. As I began to read the evening portion for June 19th, God really spoke to me.

Gold tried in the fire

"There is no man that hath left house, or brethren, or sisters, or father, or mother, or wife, or children, or lands, for my sake, and the gospel's, but he shall receive an hundredfold now in this time, houses and brethren, and sisters, and mothers and children, and lands, with persecutions; and in the world to come eternal life.

Beloved, think it not strange concerning the fiery trial which is to try you, as though some strange thing happened unto you. — Now for a season, if need be, ye are in heaviness through manifold temptations: that the trial of your faith, being much more precious than of gold that perisheth, though it be tried with fire, might be found unto praise and honour and glory at the appearing of Jesus Christ.

The God of all grace, who hath called us unto his eternal glory by Christ Jesus, after that ye have suffered a while, make you perfect, stablish, strengthen, settle you. — In the world ye shall have tribulation: but be of good cheer; I have overcome the world. (Rev. 3:18; Mark 10:29,30; 1 Pet. 4:12; 1 Pet. 1:6,7, 1 Pet. 5:10; John 16:33)"

With tears streaming down my cheeks, I got out of my mosquito net, tore up my letter of resignation and threw it away. In the weeks to come I didn't feel any better physically, but I knew God was with me and things would work out for my good.

Next, I had to learn to get along with my colleagues. I thought I was pretty easy to get along with, but then I had chosen my friends carefully.

Anyone who rubbed me the wrong way, I simply avoided. But you can't avoid someone if you are placed in the same house! When I moved up-country, I prayed, "Lord, I'm willing to live with anyone, except Sue." In His wisdom, Sue and I were both sent to live in the town of Paknampho. In working through this relationship, God gave me great respect and love for Sue and we became good friends. Since joining OMF I have had nineteen different housemates. Although some of these relationships have not been easy, I do thank God for each one and for what I have learned from them.

Finally, I had to learn to be obedient. Six months before my first furlough, our Director for Thailand came to visit us. We were all wondering why he had come until he said, "Diane, can I talk with you?" He then shared that there was a desperate need at Chefoo School for a dorm auntie. Would I be willing to fill that need? This time, after much prayer, I said yes, and within a week I was in the Cameron Highlands.

I had been told that my responsibility would be ten junior girls, but on arriving, I discovered to my horror that I would be caring for seventeen junior boys.

Right from the beginning, my reservations about a boarding school were torn to shreds. The children were happy and it was a loving, caring, united community. To my surprise, my health improved drastically. After several weeks of adjustment, I began thoroughly to enjoy and love the place, the staff and especially "my boys."

As the busy days flew by, I felt that perhaps God would have me return to Chefoo after my furlough, but I wanted to be absolutely sure that this was His will. So one morning after the boys had gone to school, while I was having my Quiet Time, I asked God if He wanted me at Chefoo to have John, our principal, approach me about it that very day. I finished my Quiet Time and went out to pick some flowers for my room. The first person I bumped into was John who greeted me with, "Diane, I've been looking for you. Do you have time for a wee (he is Irish!) chat with me?" When we sat down in his office, John looked at me and said, "Diane, I have nothing specific to talk to you about, but in my Quiet Time this morning God told me that you have something you wanted to share with me. Do you?" I could hardly contain myself when I realized that John had his Quiet Time at 7 a.m. and I hadn't had mine until 9 a.m. How wonderfully God works!

I gladly shared with John my desire to return to Chefoo after furlough if there would be a place for me. He readily assured me that I would find a welcome at Chefoo and could either continue to be a dorm auntie or join the teaching staff. As furlough was so near, I decided to wait to consult my parents and home church before I came to a final decision.

When I arrived home, everyone enthusiastically approved changing my place of work to Chefoo School, so I returned the following year as the grade one teacher. Grade one has always been my favourite and there was an opening in that very area just the term I was officially joining the staff.

My years at Chefoo have been the happiest and the most fulfilling of my life. God has poured out His Spirit on our valley bringing joy, love and a sense of His presence to both the children and the staff. It is with a grateful heart that I can now say, "Thank you, Lord, for sending me to Chefoo!"

Maria Herren *from Switzerland, joined OMF in 1964.*

Heart's Desire

IS GOD INTERESTED in romances? Do romances happen in OMF? Where does God's guidance come in? Here is a story which shows that God *is* interested in romances, that He *does* guide and that He honours those who commit this important area of their life into His safe and trustworthy hands.

In a beautiful place in the heart of Europe, I grew up as the youngest of seven children of loving Christian parents. One beautiful autumn Saturday in 1963, the colours of the leafy trees surrounding our farmhouse had already turned into golden yellows and the windows were graced with heavily blooming geraniums. Unusual activity was going on inside and outside the house — we were cleaning, baking, cooking and decorating for Sunday, which would bring many friends and relatives to our home for a special farewell. It was to be the valedictory service of one of my brothers, who was about to sail for Singapore only a few days later as a new OMF missionary.

But why was I so excited about it all? After all, it was not I who was the centre of attention — I still had six months to go until my turn came. But my brother would not be the only missionary candidate speaking at the church and celebrating his farewell with us. Another young man would be with him, who would also be joining him on the long trip to Singapore. The two had already toured the churches for some weeks giving their testimonies and saying their goodbyes. In past days my brother had deliberately dropped remarks about his friend in my hearing so he could watch my reaction — but he was not going to get any.

As I helped with preparations my mind went back to my Bible School training in London. Occasionally I would get up at night to stand in front of the window and gaze into the starry sky that looked down on the huge city that housed someone I had briefly seen just once some years ago. How I would have liked to see him again! And how easy it would have been to attend the OMF prayer meeting in London, to which I used to go when my brother was on the OMF candidates course. But I would not, lest he might think I had my eye on him. And now I could not escape seeing him and was very glad of it! Little did I realize this was to be a meeting that a higher hand had organized.

I do not remember much of the service the next day, but I do remember the great fellowship we had around the dinner table at my home. And there was that handsome young fellow sitting next to my brother! I had a hard time not to look too often in his direction, but in spite of trying hard our eyes did happen to meet a few times. Were we trying to guess each other's thoughts?

That evening I overheard a remark of an eighty-year-old aunt when she said to someone in parting, "Have you noticed that young man's eyes? I would not be surprised if he had set them on a member of this household."

I thank the Lord not only for nice celebrations but also for the cleaning up session afterwards, for it was then we got a first chance to talk together. There was even a time that Monday morning when we were left alone on the job. We did not worry too much about the cleaning anymore, but were deeply interested in hearing each other's story of how the Lord had led us to Bible School and then to OMF. The time was all too short, but long enough for a quiet assurance to start growing in our hearts that one day our lives would touch again.

Six months later I was in a group of 24 new workers sailing towards Singapore. The closer we got to Singapore the greater was our anticipation. How soon would we find out to which country each of us was going? Could we trust the Lord that He would overrule in this? In those days designations were not talked about until after a new missionary's arrival in Singapore, when each would meet with the directors. If someone felt led to a certain country or type of work this was often taken into consideration, but on the whole it was up to the directors to make the decision.

Can you imagine what we went through those first few days in Singapore? There were as many hopes and dreams as there were members in our group. Everyone felt the growing tension as the moment when our designations would be announced came closer.

Hundreds of miles away someone else was beginning to feel that tension also. More than once over the past few weeks the thought had come to him that really there would be nothing wrong in letting the directors in Singapore know that he was rather interested in a young lady in the group of new workers about to arrive there. Or should he even go one step further and write to the girl he loved and help things along in this way? But no, a long time ago he had firmly committed the whole matter to the Lord, fully expecting Him to do what really was such a small thing for Him — clearly to guide the directors in their decision, and bring the one he loved to the same country and to the same people.

The evening before we were told about our designation I slipped quietly on my knees at my bedside. My heart was in turmoil. "Lord," I said, "was it right for me to tell the directors that I had an open mind about my future ... that they could send me wherever they felt was right for me, when really deep down in my heart I very much desired to be sent to one country only?"

My heart went out to the one I had loved ever

since we first met at home. "Lord, can I trust you that you will overrule in that all-important matter of my designation?" That night my Bible reading took me to Psalm 20. As I came to verse 4 it was as if the Lord Himself was speaking to me. "The Lord grant you according to your own heart, and fulfil all your counsel." While I was reading the Lord's promise over and over again my burden was lifted, giving place to an overwhelming assurance that the Lord was going to send me to the country of my heart's desire.

Little did I know that while I was praying, struggling and finally coming to the place of assurance, the directors had called an extra meeting to talk and pray once more about my designation, as they did not really have peace of mind yet about it.

The next morning emotions were running high as one after another filed out of the directors' offices having been told the country of their designation. There were tears of joy as friends who could stay together embraced each other, and tears of sorrow of those who knew they would have to part. Hardly an eye stayed dry.

As for me and my future, everything seemed to have hinged on that special meeting the directors had called the night before. During that time they were led to change the designation they had anticipated for me to the country of my heart's desire!

From then on I knew that the one I loved was waiting for me at the other end. And so it was!

Gay Pye *and Terry, from UK, have been in Korea with OMF since 1977.*

*I could never do that with **my** children*

"HOW WILL YOU FEEL about sending your children off to school in Japan when they are six?" asked OMF Home Director John Wallis in his quiet way. Of course we knew of others who had done this, but how we ourselves would feel ... well, how do you answer that question when the said children are only a handful of months old? "What are the alternatives?" I remember one of us asking. John mentioned some other possible courses of action, but then stressed, "OMF's Chefoo School is the norm." "Well," we said, "*if* we go to Korea, we'll face that bridge when we come to it." After all, did not the Lord Himself tell us not to be anxious about tomorrow?

We came. Our two children of a handful of months soon became three, and the months became years. And overnight, or so it seemed, the quiet question became relevant. The timing of our first furlough was such that Elizabeth, our oldest, turned six just seven months before we were due to go home. Elizabeth was well aware that she would probably be going to Chefoo. Our colleagues' children were already there, and the pattern of coming and going was familiar to her. Aware that if still in England she would by now be in her second year at school, and strongly encouraged by my husband Terry, I had been trying for some months to teach her the rudiments of the three Rs. It was hard work, and if that was really one of the viable alternatives to Chefoo both she and I were becoming rapidly disillusioned with it.

The point was that, although we had talked about her going to Chefoo, firmly in our minds and hers was the fixed idea that she would not go until after furlough. What was more, we were in the throes of trying out a Korean kindergarten, though admittedly with limited success. Shortly after the above-mentioned sixth birthday, Peter Pattisson our superintendent shared with us that he and his wife Audrey felt that Elizabeth was ready to go to Chefoo for one term before furlough.

We were about to go for three weeks' holiday to the beach, so we agreed to think and pray about it. We did so, and also broached the subject with Elizabeth herself, but she adamantly insisted that she should only go after furlough. We returned from the beach with a negative response.

Our Elizabeth and small Peter Deane had always been close, but then Peter had gone off to Chefoo. As is the way sometimes, Elizabeth transferred her affections to Matthew, the next one down and only a few months younger. That summer there was some thought of Matthew going to Chefoo a little earlier than usual. One afternoon in August, Elizabeth and I talked about this together.

"Mummy, I would like to go to school with Matthew." And the rest of the afternoon so revolved around school that she had me at the airport seeing her off, wondering where I was going to get labels to sew on her clothes, and how we were going to tell the kindergarten that she wouldn't be coming back. Terry came home later to be greeted with, "Daddy, I'm going to school with Matthew." And with bubbling enthusiasm she chattered away.

As Terry saw that she was really intent on going, a week of gloom settled on our home. It is one thing to say you will face it when it comes, but when it *does* come the true unwillingness in our hearts comes to the fore. So passed a week of Elizabeth bubbling, me praying and Terry wrestling. And I saw a miracle. I saw the Lord's peace take over and Terry able to come to terms with the coming separation. It was as if the Lord was saying to us, "I gave you a chance to do my will but you somehow missed it. So now I have bypassed you and given your child a heart to go."

I guess we shall never forget the first day she went to school. Isn't it a day that every mother remembers? A friend of mine, whose kitchen window overlooked the school playground, tells of her relief when, looking out during playtime that first day, she saw her five year old having fun with the others. And how many mothers have walked home from the school, two blocks away, with hearts like lead and lumps in their throats? We shared all those feelings, only a yawning gap of fourteen weeks stretched between that first day and "hometime". Our small daughter, clutching a two-foot rag doll, comforted me, "It's all right, Mummy, Jesus is with us." And her last words as she went through immigration, "I love you, Mummy," and a bright smile. And then in a letter several weeks later, "Me being here at school in Japan is my way of helping you and Daddy be missionaries."

This special guidance concerning schooling was so important when we went on furlough. With the best will in the world, so many Christians find it hard to accept that this separation of young children from their parents could be God's will. Most of us have at some time or other had the comment, "I could never do that with *my* children". The underlying implication seems to be, "therefore you don't love *your* children as much as I love *mine*" and that can hurt an already badly aching heart. How thankful we were on furlough to have been through the experience already, and our constant testimony was, "No, we didn't send Elizabeth away to school. We had to *let* her go." Elizabeth herself was our best aid as she chatted happily about Chefoo, even to her very reluctant Granny! So, the "when we get back we are going to have to send the children away to school" spectre was unable to haunt us even though the thought of it sometimes made our hearts sink.

We have learnt some valuable lessons through that first experience and subsequent ones. It is better to face a thing squarely and fairly and then you are better able to help those around you do the same (for instance, grandparents). At the same time we have learnt that truly, truly the Lord's grace is sufficient when the time comes, but He does not have too much grace to spare if we insist on being anxious. After all, he has told us *not* to be anxious and therefore He does not promise that His grace is sufficient for our every *anxiety*, but for our every *need*.

In a year or so's time we have to make another big decision regarding schooling. I hope we don't make the wrong decision, but having seen the Lord bypass us once, maybe He will do it again if we choose wrongly. For one thing is sure; if we have known the Lord's grace in our hearts as parents, we have been wide-eyed to see it in our children's lives as, term by term, with courage and poise, they get on the aeroplane back to school.

Elizabeth's first letter from school this term began, "Thank you for all the lovely times we had in the holidays. I miss you and love you a lot, but we are having such a fun time back at school."

Follow through on guidance received

Rosemary Chandler *from USA, has been a member of OMF since 1965.*

God's Way Is Perfect

WHILE I WAS training to be a nurse I started dating Art, a medical student who also felt God leading him toward medical work with OMF. Together we prayed about God's will for our lives. During the two years of our courtship we met OMF missionary Mary Teegardin and as a result our interest in Saiburi hospital and the Muslim work in the south of Thailand grew.

A year after we were married, Art was attending a summer seminary course and I was working at the local hospital. After work one day we went for a swim. I was tired and only stayed in the water a short time, before coming out to talk with some of the other wives. A few minutes later I looked for Art and couldn't find him. Then started the nightmare of calling for the lifeguard. They found his body and started artificial respiration, we called a doctor who injected his heart, but it was too late. God had taken him home.

Then the doubts and questions came flooding in.

Why had God allowed this? Men and doctors were needed overseas. Why couldn't it have been me instead? Friends asked, "Will you still go overseas?" My school of nursing offered me a teaching post and an opportunity to work on my master's degree. But life seemed worthless just then. As the "Why's" kept coming, God gave me Amy Carmichael's words, "In acceptance lieth peace", and Psalm 18:30,32, "As for God, His way is perfect ... He maketh my way perfect." Although there was anger at God to begin with and yes, even thoughts that life was not worth living and I might as well commit suicide ... in the end the prayers of so many of God's people upheld me and I came to know that He still had a purpose for my life.

God had called and this was not dependent on whether I was married or single. So I applied to OMF and attended the fall candidates course. There were many tears and the evil monster of self pity had to be constantly fought. But God had called and so I went ahead.

Now, 18 years later, I'm so thankful to the Lord for all the way He has led. This has included work among nurses in the Philippines for six years, until God graciously gave me another life partner. Since 1972, Ken and I have been involved in church planting. God has given us two lovely adopted children — but that's another story.

Jean Anderson *from Ireland, has worked in Thailand since 1953.*

A
Listening
Ear

THE SECOND WORLD WAR was over at last. I had finished nurses' training and was spending an extra year doing district midwifery. What was the next step? How could I know for sure that God had called me to work with the China Inland Mission? Perhaps it was only a romantic idea — the result of reading the life of Hudson Taylor and other CIM books.

I searched the pages of *China's Millions* as the magazine was then called, and especially the testimonies of new workers, to try and find an answer to this burning question. Should I leave my nursing job and apply to Bible School, or should I apply directly to the Mission?

Finally I asked the Lord to give me a definite word of Scripture on the matter. His answer to my prayer was printed in bold type on the front page of the next copy of the magazine, "This is the way, walk ye in it." (Isa. 30:21). The same verse came in my daily Scripture Union portion on the day that I received the magazine. This incident taught me that the Lord will confirm His guidance from His Word when we ask Him. In 35 years I have never been left in doubt about His will when I definitely sought it, was willing to do it and asked Him for Scriptural information.

Once I had been accepted as a candidate for work in China, I had imagined that I would not require guidance on any major issue again, or at least not for a very long time. How wrong I was!

Before I had finished my two years of Bible training China had been overrun by Communists and the entire missionary body was forced to evacuate. My call to the CIM was tested for three years; during that time I worked with the London City Mission, in health visiting and with Crusaders. All of that experience proved invaluable when I finally arrived as a missionary in Thailand with the OMF.

During those three years I was not lacking friends who urged me to go to Africa, Nepal or India. I even made tentative inquiries about work in Nepal, but there was no clear leading from the Lord that any of these places was His will for me. So I learned to wait — something I have never found easy and which I was going to have to learn again and again.

When the OMF team surveying the needs of Thailand submitted their report I was sent a copy. As I read it I knew that the Lord was saying once again, "This is the way." Confirmation came when I received a letter from the Home Director asking me if I would be willing to go to Thailand in a few months' time.

As we six new workers sat on the deck of the little steamer from Singapore one Sunday morning in August 1953 we had our first glimpse of Thailand — the broad muddy river, the banks lined with thick vegetation which was still wet from the previous night's heavy rain, the little temples with their orange-tiled roofs and gold leaf adornment glinting in the early morning sun, and the villagers paddling small boats near the banks. I opened my Bible and found in that day's portion the wonderful promise, "Lift up thine eyes and look ... for all the land that thou seest, to thee will I give it and to thy seed for ever" (Gen. 13:14-15). It was over five years since I had asked for the Lord's guidance concerning my future service for Him, and the way that He had chosen for me was opening up at last.

I had expected to spend my life in Thailand ... but now what was God saying to me? During my second term I contracted polio in the medical clinic where I was working in Central Thailand. The Lord wonderfully guided our Superintendent's wife to ask help from some American servicemen in flying me out to Bangkok. She herself had contracted polio in China and had been unable to get out of her station because of heavy rains and impassable roads. She knew I would find fifteen miles by boat and then over sixty miles in the back of a car very difficult, so she went to see the Christian men who had asked her husband to conduct Bible studies for them. They were very glad to help, and within an hour had landed their helicopter in front of the government offices in Inburi. It caused quite a stir and hundreds of people came to see us off. We reached Bangkok in half an hour — the boat and car journey would have taken five or six!

I found that God guides even when we don't know what to ask. After I had spent nearly two months in Bangkok Christian Hospital, a young British Army doctor was able to arrange for my transport home on an RAF hospital plane, one of six stretcher cases. This meant that I did not need an escort, and it was a great deal cheaper than a commercial flight where I would have required six seats.

It was to be four years before I would fly back to Thailand again — four years of hospital and physiotherapy, adapting to life in a wheelchair and learning to drive a hand-controlled car. The conviction that God still wanted me in Thailand had never left me, though I seldom talked about returning as most people responded with a knowing smile — they thought it was a crazy idea but didn't want to say so. However, not everyone thought it was crazy or impossible. As my assurance about it grew I heard that Dr Chris Maddox was willing to have me back in Manorom Christian Hospital, so I asked the Lord to confirm it if this was His plan for me. He gave me Judges 6:14, "Go in this thy strength; have not I sent thee?"

God's timing is always perfect. I applied for a permanent Thai residence visa and was granted it.

A few months later no permanent visas would be issued in London. A quota system was introduced and all new missionaries had to leave the country every two months until they acquired a permanent visa. This often took several years and I could not have coped with the travel involved.

My burden was to do evangelism amongst the hospital patients and their relatives, but for a number of years I was involved in the leprosy work. I had learned some simple lab techniques while I was home in Ireland and was able to set up the lab work in the leprosy wing and finally to train a Thai man to take and read skin smears. I was also a "filler in" when doctor or nurse were away. In my heart I had rebelled against going into medical work during my first term, but had not done so openly. Psalm 106:15, "He gave them their request, but sent leanness into their souls," had always acted as a brake and I could not forget the warnings given to me as a candidate about not missing God's will by refusing to accept a designation given by the Mission leaders. Finally the way did open for me to do full-time evangelism, but I have never regretted waiting until God's time had come.

To have Thai fellow workers on the evangelistic team was something we aimed for and prayed for. Over the years several young people studying in Bible school came to us, but we found that they were too young and inexperienced for hospital work. We needed a mature Christian man, but where would we find him? Various candidates were suggested, but in each case I had no conviction that he was God's choice. One day a fellow missionary from the North told me that Mr Surapon was seeking a change and might be interested in working with us at Manorom Christian Hospital. I knew Surapon and had taught him when he worked for the leprosy control team. I had the inner assurance that he was God's man to come and join us. He has proved to be the right man for the job and I am glad I resisted other offers of service.

Miss Amnuay came to us in quite a different way. She was sent to us during the summer holiday from Bangkok Bible College because she had contracted mild tuberculosis. The doctor said she could work but we had no suitable job for her, so I was asked if I could use her in ward evangelism. There was no time to think about it, but I agreed as it was only for a couple of months. During that time I found she had a real gift for personal evangelism. She had been a practical nurse at Saiburi Hospital so was at home in a hospital, and was old enough to enter into patients' problems. By the time she returned to college we had decided to ask her to spend her intern year with us, and later to join us permanently.

Guidance is something I need fresh every morning — which patients to see first? What to say? What illustration to use? Often in response to an SOS prayer the Lord has given me a new illustration which has enabled the patient to understand what I have been trying to tell him about the Gospel. How wonderful then to hear him say, "Now I see it!" Often I have been guided to see a very sick patient at just the right moment. One man was dying of cancer and I went into his room and led him to faith in Christ when his visitors had just left. We had just finished praying when the nurses came to move him to a large ward; after that someone came to put up a drip; his relatives came back and the following day took him home. I "happened" to get there during the one brief hour when he was alone and able to talk. He went home assured that he would go straight to heaven.

One lady had been with us for two months recovering from a very serious gunshot wound. Again I "happened" to get there when the doctor told her she could go home. I was able to rejoice with her and ask her how she planned to thank God for her miraculous recovery. This conversation enabled Mr Surapon to lead her to Christ. I had to hurry off to see another woman who would not recover, but who also trusted the Saviour that same day.

The right use of money given to us can often be a real problem. When my hand-controlled car got old, a small prayer group in Ireland wrote and offered to buy me a new one. I was overwhelmed by their generosity but wrote back telling them that the import tax was 152% of cost. They were still willing to pay the entire cost, but I felt it incumbent on me to try and get the car into Thailand tax free, as the British Embassy had told me there was a special low rate for vehicles for disabled people. I filled in the forms, the car arrived, but we made no progress. I was determined not to pay out the

Lord's money unless it was absolutely necessary. After several weeks I was growing quite discouraged. The new car was sitting in the open exposed to the tropical sun and that was not doing it any good. One morning I was reading Romans, using the Living Bible, when the Lord told me clearly what to do from Romans 13:7, "Pay your taxes and import duties gladly." Later we found out the special tax rate did not cover cars. I had never known that verse was in the Bible!

It is now 35 years since I first began to seek for God's guidance in matters large and small. I have learned two things. First, I will always need His guidance, and second, I will always hear that voice behind me saying, "This is the way, walk ye in it," so long as I keep a listening ear.

Doris Elsaesser who comes from Germany, joined OMF in 1966.

The Offering Of Thanksgiving

I HAD HAD ENOUGH. For twelve years I had been labouring in church planting and leadership training with the Iraya tribe of Mindoro, Philippines, together with my husband Hermann. We had been childless for most of the year since Samuel, the youngest of our three children, had started boarding school more than two years ago. Now we were home on furlough in Germany, and I was enjoying being an ordinary housewife and mother. I had my moments, of course, when I felt a gnawing uneasiness about not fulfilling the Great Commission, about not being involved with people, with teaching, with counselling. But these moments would pass.

Now was the time, I felt, to settle down at home, looking for a ministry in our own land, which to me seemed more non-Christian than anything I had encountered in the Philippines. If Hermann would be finished with deputation meetings and get started in some kind of church work, I could become involved again and find my niche as well as caring for my family. I would be content and fulfilled.

The last few years had been especially hard. The decade-old struggle between the tribal people and intruders from all over the Philippines had intensified, and we had been caught in the middle of it. All the members of one of our churches had been accused of "squatting" on their own land! It happened that they did not have legal title to it, as they had no knowledge of legal procedures. We got embroiled in this and Hermann had suffered arrest and considerable psychological harrassment. It had been a hard, exhausting year, and the fear that something like it might happen again had stayed with me. And also the fear that we would not achieve anything, that we could not change the system; and the fear that standing up for the rights of minorities does them no good; and the fear of watching our beloved Iraya friends and brothers suffer indignities and maltreatment without being able to help them; and the fear of not seeing any success while trying to improve their lot.

Another thought was troubling me too. I am a nurse, and had always felt responsible when someone was ill. If a patient died, I had to fight the idea that it was I who had killed him, through negligence and ignorance. I knew this was silly, but caring for the sick was a burden I would have liked to discard.

And what about church work these last twelve years? Was it not all a string of disappointments?

We had watched keen Christians backsliding, marriages breaking up, people not listening to our advice; in spite of our encouragement personal Bible reading was not widely practised, sins were not dealt with, and some churches were soundly asleep.

It seemed I had forgotten all the bright experiences: people giving up their spirit practices and becoming new men and women in Christ; churches coming into being where before there were none, through our efforts and those of our Iraya brothers; Sunday Schools started where formerly the children were growing up without any knowledge of God our Creator and Jesus Christ our Redeemer.

Now we had been on furlough for eight months. I felt it was about time to ask for leave of absence, to start looking round for a place where we could serve the Lord in our own country. I didn't mean to resign from missionary work. Sometime in the future we might well be able to return to the Philippines. But not now.

I broached the subject to Hermann. Yes, he too felt it would be wise and right to stay in Germany, to make a home for our teenage children. But not now, not yet. The children could continue with their education at the German school in Singapore, well cared for at the OMF hostel there and joining us during their holidays. Our job with the Iraya churches was not yet finished. Our call to serve the Lord in the Philippines was still valid. He had not replaced it with a different call. So, why not one more term before settling at home?

It sounded so right and straightforward, but I couldn't face it. To me it felt all wrong. What business of mine were the troubles of the Iraya over their land? What could I do about their ailments? How could I help their struggling churches, their evangelizing of heathen tribesmen? How little success we had seen when trying to straighten out erring believers. I was not needed there. It was all the Lord's business. He was responsible for carrying on in the hills of Mindoro.

I started pleading with Him, "Lord, you surely don't want me to go to Mindoro for the fourth time. I'm not really all that useful there, you know (as if He didn't know ...). Just show us the next step to take here in our home land. There must be a place somewhere around here for us, a slot we can fill." Just to convince the Lord that I was really serious, I set Him a deadline: "One month from now, Lord, we need to know the next step. And one other thing: Please bring Hermann around too, that he can see that *now* is the time for us to stay at home."

Two things were in my mind — I wanted to be in the centre of our Father's will for our lives; and I could not face another term in the Philippines. I continued pleading. I begged, I cried, I implored. But there was no sign or sound from my Father.

The days passed, and I became panicky. Would God let me down? Would He just ignore my plea? I shrank from becoming hurt through disappointment. I was convinced that it would be easy for the Lord either to guide us to some sphere of service in our home land, or — if there was really and truly no

way of escape — to fill me with peace and new joy
for another term as an overseas missionary.

But the month was up, and no answer had
arrived, neither a call to a ministry at home nor
peace about leaving. I have sometimes wondered
about bargaining with the Lord. Who are we, after
all, to set deadlines for the Almighty God? Does it
upset Him? Surely not ... but I wonder.

There have been occasions when I have asked for
something specific to be granted at a certain time,
and the Lord has wonderfully responded. For
example, once it was necessary to have a talk with a
believer whom we had not seen for several weeks.
He lived some 15 km away and was rather difficult
to contact. So I asked the Lord to send him to us
before the week was over — and He did!

Another occasion makes me smile when I think of
it. The ironing in our part of the Philippines is done
with charcoal, and the "charcoal lady" lived some
distance away and came round with her wares
every few months. When we had just about finished
the previous sackful, I asked the Lord to please
send the vendor before we ran out. Two days later
she appeared at our gate. How thrilled she was
when I told her she was an answer to prayer!

But now ... surely we had done what we could to
build God's church among the Iraya. Someone else
should take over. Why didn't God listen to me? He
ignored my pleas and didn't bother about my
deadline. I was deeply hurt. Did it not matter to my
heavenly Father how I felt? Was it fair just to ignore
me?

At this time we went for a short holiday at our former Bible College high up in the mountains in Switzerland. By the hour I would sit and gaze at the beautiful panorama of Eiger, Mönch and Jungfrau across the lake of Thun. All the while I was pleading for the burden to lift, either for peace and joy for a new term or for God's call to a new assignment.

Nothing happened, except that I fetched a book from the library to take my thoughts off my problem. And, sure enough, it was the story of a missionary lady who didn't like it on the mission field! She was given two Bible verses: Joshua 1:9 and Psalm 50:23. Luther renders Joshua 1:9, "I have commanded you, be joyful and of good courage." Can God command a person to be joyful? I was not too sure how to handle this. But it seemed to me that I didn't need to sit and wait until joy arrived. I should be of good courage right away because of God's promises. And then the other words, "He who brings an offering of praise and thanksgiving honours and glorifies me." Offering means giving something away. It might even hurt. Well, it might mean saying thank you for difficult things. Did I need to say thank you for being sent back to the Philippines? Did I need to give up my grumblings and fears and protests, and replace them with joy and good courage?

I realized for the first time that I had been untrue to myself when I said I wanted to do my Father's will whatever it was. I had *not* been ready to accept His will if it meant another term overseas. So I had to ask for forgiveness. And He cleansed me and took over once more.

It would not be correct to say that from then on I was looking forward to our next term; or that I was happy. It was rather a quiet confidence in my heart that I was doing the right thing. And thanking for it made it easier.

At last the day of our departure arrived. The last farewells were said and we boarded the plane. Then it happened. High over the Alps, peace and joy flooded me like a river. I could have danced! I was on my way to the place the Lord wanted me to go, in order to do the work He wanted me to do!

Act in accordance with the Word of God

Tim Symonds *and Zinnia joined OMF in 1981, and now work in Hong Kong.*

The Service of the House of the Lord

AFTER I HAD spent eight years in the British Army, with Christian witness playing a prominent part in my thinking and activities, I found I was experiencing an increasing tension between the competing claims on my time of Christian activities and my profession. I began to pray about whether I should remain in the army indefinitely. About that time a notice appeared on my desk about vacancies for language training at the Ministry of Defence Chinese Language School in Hong Kong. I sat up and thought, "If I did leave the Army and became a missionary one day, it would be useful to have a language qualification." I decided to try the door and see if it opened. It did.

When I reached Hong Kong God spoke to me through a verse in my daily reading:

"Be strong and of a good courage, and do it: fear not, nor be dismayed: for the Lord God ... will not fail you nor forsake you until you

have finished all the work for the service of
the house of the Lord" (1 Chron. 28:20)

I needed that promise over the next two and a
half arduous years of the course, and I wondered
how and when the language would be used in the
"service of the house of the Lord." I believed that
while I was in the Army the Army was my mission
field and I should not go looking for opportunities
for witness elsewhere. And I was obliged to remain
in the Army for five years after completing the
course.

Meanwhile, before I completed the course the
Lord had led me to my life-partner. Lest I should
give the impression that the signposts of my
guidance have always been immediately crystal
clear, I must say that in the matter of "walking
out", as in other matters, I lost my way on
occasions. It is also true, however, that God has
used my mistakes to show me the course I should be
taking. When my life-partner-to-be came to stay at
my parents' home before we were engaged, on the
first morning of her visit I read in *Daily Light*, "I
will give them one heart and one way ... for the
good of them and of their children after them"
(Jeremiah 32:39). The significance of this struck me
and when I mentioned it to my prized guest she
said she had read the same passage and been
similarly impressed! We believed the Lord's hand
was in our union and "exchanged contracts" before
she left.

Several years of marriage passed, but to our distress no children appeared. We began to realize that God was putting us through a trial of faith, and longed for comfort and reassurance. We recalled that the verse we had read on our engagement had included children and believed the Lord would not have mentioned children if He had meant us to be childless. He did reassure us, for in the years that followed when our faith seemed to be at a low ebb we heard Him speaking to us through verses such as "Let patience have her perfect work" (James 1:4) and "He who did not spare His own Son, but gave Him up for us all — how will He not also, along with Him, graciously give us all things?" (Romans 8:32)

As time progressed we wondered if the Lord's word referred to adoption so we tried exploring this avenue. But our efforts met with difficulties which caused us to lose our peace and made us sense that this was not the Lord's will for us. So we left the matter with God, our peace returned and not long afterwards the miracle happened — conception! The timing was interesting — we had waited seven years, the baby was born in the seventh month of the year and she weighed 7 lbs 7 oz! God's perfect touch was evident. Then, having held my wife's hand during the birth it was a nice comment to read in the *Daily Light* passage for the day when I turned into bed in the small hours, "Two are better than one for they have a good reward for their labour" (Eccl.4:9)!

Between our marriage and the arrival of our baby, God had given us fresh guidance about our way forward. The Army told me that because of Defence cuts I would be made redundant with two years notice. I had been looking for a green light to leave the Army and this was it. The Lord confirmed it by causing us to come across the same verse of Scripture in the space of about a fortnight in four different contexts. First my wife returned from a meeting at which she had learned a new chorus. It ran:

> "He sent me to preach the good news to the poor,
> Tell prisoners that they are prisoners no more,
> Tell blind people that they can see,
> And set the downtrodden free."

A day or two later our daily reading contained the verse from Isaiah 61 from which these words come; the third occasion was when, after spending a special time in prayer about our future, I felt directed to our calendar and the text for the day was again Isaiah 61:1. And finally, when we attended a church service a few days later the same words were looking at us from the head of the service sheet!

After two years with a forces-related Christian organization and then a year helping Vietnamese refugees — when my Cantonese began to be used "for the service of the house of the Lord" — we heard a sermon on the call to personal ministry which seemed directed to us. Our ministry up till then had embraced personal work but had been mainly administrative. We tested this call to preach by applying for ordination in the Church of England, but the door did not open and again we wondered if we had misheard.

As we prayed further, the sense that we were meant to be prepared to move persisted. Attempts to buy a house met with failure. Then one day our copy of OMF's magazine *East Asia Millions* arrived and my wife's eye was arrested by an item which ran, "Pray for workers to do church planting in Hong Kong." About the same time we received a letter from the OMF Home Director, with whom we had shared our situation, mentioning the same need. This went straight to our hearts. Then we read a treasured promise, "Delight yourself in the Lord and He will give you the desires of your heart" (Psalm 37:4). The mist was lifting, the signposts were becoming clearer, and sure enough the way to Hong Kong with the OMF opened up for us. A further confirmation of the Lord's will was that when I mentioned to a colleague the need for someone to succeed me in my job she thought of the ideal person straight away.

To be returning to the Far East "in the service of the house of the Lord" seemed like a dream coming true. Being prepared to uproot ourselves along the way had not always been easy. It had been tempting to cling to the ground we knew rather than explore the unknown, but the experiences of God's guidance had made our willingness to change direction immeasurably worthwhile. God really does guide those who learn to listen to Him, as He promises: "Whether you turn to the right or to the left, your ears will hear a voice behind you saying, This is the way, walk in it" (Isaiah 30:21).

Anne Ruck *and John, from UK, joined OMF in 1978.*

All A Ghastly Mistake?

PUSHING OUR CAR brought on my first miscarriage.

I was on my own late at night, driving back to All Nations Christian College after a weekend of praise and renewal at our home church in Birmingham. John had had college commitments, but I was glad that I had been free to share in such a stimulating time of learning and fellowship; glad too of the opportunity to proclaim my newly pregnant condition. From under the car somewhere came a strange clonking sound. At first I dismissed it. "Trust God for travelling mercies," I told myself; and then a little later, "Better just take a look." I drew up under a street light and lifted the bonnet. But the open bonnet cut out the light, so I gave a shove, and pushed the car backwards a foot or so. This enabled me to scrutinize, in complete incomprehension, the radiator, starter motor, whatsit and thingummy (my mechanical skills are nil), before slamming down the bonnet and driving quite calmly a further eighty miles.

Next day the bleeding began. For the first time it came home to me fully, with a shock, that I had been carrying another, new life within me. And had lost it.

The second miscarriage, again at nine weeks so technically an abortion, came almost, if painfully, as a relief, absolving me from the yet unresolved guilt of the first. The hospital staff, kind and efficient, suggested blood tests and X-rays to discover the cause. All proved negative.

As I lay in bed expecting my third miscarriage in the space of a year, the Lord began gently to teach me. On the wall was a poster, blue-white; a skeletal tree in a bleak and snowbound land. "Faith is the assurance of things hoped for, the conviction of things not seen." The text was Hebrews 11:1. Our vicar had preached on it last Sunday. "Faith," he had said, "believes, in spite of all the evidence to the contrary." Like Abraham, who lived always just a foreigner in the land promised to his descendants. Like Shadrack, Meshack and Abednego, *before* they knew that God would deliver them from the fiery furnace. "But if not, we will not serve your gods or worship the golden image which you have set up." Their trust in God was sure whatever the outcome. As the pains began, and the threatened became the inevitable, I sang:

> "Help me to walk aright,
> More by faith, less by sight,

Into Thy perfect light,
Teach me Thy way."

This time chromosome tests were suggested for
both of us. The gynaecologist pointed out rather
tetchily that the National Health Service was
spending a small fortune to prove to me that I was
healthy. Again the results were negative. "There is
no earthly reason why you should not have a
perfectly normal baby next time," was the considered medical opinion of numerous doctors as we
left England in February 1978 to join the OMF
Orientation Course in Singapore. We were following what we believed to be the Lord's calling,
confirmed by our church and the OMF, to serve
Him in Indonesia.

I had my fourth miscarriage that October in
Malaysia.

Visas for Indonesia were hard to come by. After
three months of lectures and orientation in Singapore, a small batch of missionary tadpoles were sent
to wait in the quiet backwaters of the OMF Mission
Home in Kuala Lumpur. No one knew when the
visas would be granted; meanwhile, with the help of
cassettes, books and an Indonesian teacher we
could start our language study in pleasant sur-
roundings. The local Malay language, closely
related to Indonesian, would give opportunities for
practice. No responsibilities, no home to run,
nothing to do but study, the facilities of modern
medicine close at hand. We prayed, we talked, we

asked advice, we were sure that this was God's time and place for a successful pregnancy.

Nothing was normal from the start, and the ninth and twelfth weeks were especially tense times remembering earlier disappointments. But this time we had more definitely sought God's will, and we gradually became convinced that this time He promised us healing. Mark chapter 5 thrust itself upon us at every turn. For me it was the story of Jairus's daughter which spoke; for John it was the woman with the flow of blood. So many doctors (and I had seen specialists in three different places in England) had only made her worse, but by touching Jesus' cloak she was healed. At 13 weeks I was confined to bed and the limbo of waiting.

"Should we ask someone to lay hands on me? Or announce publicly in the prayer meeting that we believe God is going to heal me?"

"Not necessary," said John. "We believe the Lord will heal you. That's what matters."

We believed. Right to the last minute I clung on to the words that Jesus had spoken to Jairus when they told him his daughter was dead: "Don't be afraid, only believe."

Only believe. Until the evidence lay unmistakably before us. Another note for my record card: spontaneous abortion at 14 weeks.

Only believe. But what was there left to believe in?

Don't, please, misunderstand me. I believed in God. Our Father's love is deep beyond knowledge, and when once we have felt His everlasting arms around us there can be no more doubting that. What had shattered was my faith in *us*, in our ability to hear and understand His voice — or perhaps yes, admit it, perhaps in His clearness (or His faithfulness?) in making His will plain. Should we have asked for laying on of hands? Was our faith too small and so God could not heal? But our faith had been sure. Had we simply been mistaken? Then how could we trust our sense of guidance in other things? What price the "guidance" which had led us through the years from reluctance to willingness to sureness; to leave home, families, jobs, security (as we thought) to face a frightening (as it seemed) unknown? We had been convinced that God would heal. He had not. We had been convinced that God was calling us to Indonesia. Six months we had been in Malaysia and still no signs of a visa. Older missionaries, passing through Kuala Lumpur, asked, "Where will you go if/when you are re-designated?" Had it all been a ghastly mistake?

New Zealand OMFer Val Sands, in her gentle wisdom, suggested that we share these feelings with a small group of prayer partners. In our home church in Birmingham there was just such a group, of caring faithful friends who met regularly to pray for us and who knew us too well to be shocked if we laid bare our doubts and fears. Their letters and prayers and concern were a lifeline. The verses they sent I have forgotten now, but their message was all the same: trust! Their advice was to wait until I could consult further medical specialists — which presumably would be when we went home on furlough in 1982. I felt comforted but a little disappointed; I had hoped for some dramatic "word from the Lord." But prophecy can sometimes wear a prosaic face.

Just after our baby would have been born (perfect timing, we would have said), our visas came through for Indonesia. We had to go first to Singapore to collect them. Beryl Anderson, who had bustled us out of lethargy often enough, and had been a tower of strength in the dark times, said that while in Singapore we must consult a Christian gynaecologist, Dr Quek, who had helped many other OMFers. I never wanted to think about doctors or babies again. It seemed clear to us now that God must not, after all, intend us to have children. But a chat with OMF's Dr Monica Hogben led to a casual phonecall on a minor connected point to Dr Quek. His immediate response was, "I think I know what might cause those symptoms." An hour later a smear was being taken for analysis.

After eleven months we had grown to love Malaysia, and to feel burdened by that country's spiritual needs. But the Indonesian visas came like a call from home. Even our introduction to Jakarta could not put us off. The stink of urine fought in our nostrils with the smell of rotting vegetables and fish. The harsh unrelenting roar of unsilenced engines, the screeching music and yelling voices blasted our ear drums. Thrusting hands and faces blocked our view of turgid waters piled high with debris, while rags and stumped-off feet and weird deformities played havoc with our consciences. But everywhere there was green — they say if you throw down a broom in Indonesian soil it will sprout leaves. And everywhere there was life; surging, sweating, laughing, loving life. And here and there we met with Indonesian Christians who had grappled with problems we may never face, and emerged with a vibrant, glowing faith that made us proud to be children of the same Father.

At an OMF prayer meeting in Jakarta, Area Director David Ellis shared his thoughts on the stilling of the storm (Mark 4). Galilean storms were spectacular. Cool air currents rushed down narrow passageways from snowcapped Mount Hermon, colliding with the hot air of Galilee's basin, 680 feet below sea level, in a frenzy of violence. The tough fishermen were used to handling this boat on this lake; but as water crashed over the side they were terrified. "We should never have come! Our guidance was all wrong!" Did some of the twelve say that? But Jesus Himself had told them to cross over the lake. Then the storm too must be part of His plan. They were awed by His power when Jesus calmed the wind and the waves. But what if they had not panicked, had lived through the storm with Jesus asleep in the boat? Certainly God's protection would have been no less.

Soon after came a letter from Singapore to say that the culture had proved positive. I had a bacterial infection. The cure? A course of antibiotics; four weeks now and a further two weeks when I became pregnant. Simple. But without that visit to Dr Quek we should never have known. And without that fourth miscarriage in Malaysia we should never have consulted Dr Quek. Our "storm" had been a necessary first part in God's healing process. What a pity I had forgotten to walk by faith!

A year later, 5th August 1980, our first child was delivered by caesarian section at Gleneagles Hospital, Singapore. I remember coming round from the anaesthetic; the urgent faces, looming large and receding, the echoing voices, some vital message that I couldn't quite grasp — then sudden meaning, "It's a boy!" A sleepy, roundfaced and beautiful baby boy. We named him Nathan — Gift of God.

And now we have two children, Nathan and Stephanie. God never gives grudgingly or by halves.

It is not always easy to come back for a second term of service, but for me the hardest one will be the third time, when we must face up to sending our children away to Chefoo School in Malaysia. I hope I shall remember that if we had never left England we should probably never have had any children. I hope I shall remember how He gave them, how in what seemed the bleakest times He was working in love. And I pray that He will enable me, when the parting seems hard, to entrust them to His care, not grudgingly but in faith. *That* will be no small miracle.

Hudson Taylor

God's Will — to Give

> Who gave Himself for our sins, that He
> might deliver us from this present evil
> world, according to the Will of God and our
> Father. *(Galatians 1:4)*

THE WILL AND PURPOSE of God is strikingly
brought before us in the Scriptures. Of our Lord
Jesus Christ we read: "Who gave Himself for our
sins, that He might deliver us from this present evil
world according to the Will of God". This great
purpose was no afterthought brought in when
Satan had marred God's beautiful creation. Far
away in the distant ages of a past eternity the Father
had one treasure — His well-beloved Son. We are
told of Him: "The Lord possessed Me in the
beginning of His way ... I was daily His delight".

To Him it was that the Father, when He created
the world, entrusted the carrying out of His glorious
design; and in Him He found One always ready to

do His will. But long ere He create man in His own image, foreseeing that His image would be marred, He purposed in His own will the redemption of the fallen race. Oh, how great was the ransom! That loved One must be given up. At such a price did God fulfil His own will. "God so loved the world, that He gave."

And then the Son of God — the object of the Father's love — how did He view this will of God? Did He empty Himself as of constraint? Nay! He "for the joy that was set before Him, endured the cross, despising the shame". He laid down His life a willing sacrifice.

Ah, how little have we entered into the spirit of the Father and of the Son! What unfaithful servants we have been! Glad to be saved at the cost of a Saviour's life, how little have we been prepared to give up our lives for His service. Is there any one of us who is free from blood-guiltiness with regard to a perishing world? It is possible to sing: "My all is on the Altar", and yet be unprepared to sacrifice a ring from one's finger, or a picture from one's wall, or a child from one's family, for the salvation of the heathen. Where is that transforming, that renewing, of our minds that makes our bodies really living sacrifices?